Abdelbaset al-Megrahi:

The Untold Story of Pan Am 103

Julio K. Ray

Copyright © 2025 by Julio K. Ray All rights reserved.

No part of this book may be reproduced, stored in a retrieval system, or transmitted in any form or by any means, electronic, mechanical, photocopying, [1] recording, scanning, or otherwise, without the prior written permission of the [2] copyright holder, except in the case of brief quotations embodied in critical reviews and certain other noncommercial uses permitted by copyright law. For permission requests, [3] please contact [4] the copyright holder or publisher.

Disclaimer

This book provides a detailed account of the Lockerbie bombing, its investigation, trial, and complex aftermath, drawing upon extensive research of public records, court proceedings, official reports, and media coverage. While every effort has been made to ensure accuracy, readers should recognise the inherent complexities involved.

The Lockerbie case remains highly controversial, with significant debate surrounding the evidence, verdict, and subsequent events. This work aims to explore these different facets and present the various perspectives – including those of the prosecution, defence, and victims' families – in a balanced way based on the available information.

Given the contested nature of many facts and interpretations, definitive answers to all questions surrounding this tragedy may remain elusive. Portrayals of the real individuals involved are based on the public record and historical accounts.

Table of Contents

Prologue: The Silence Before the Storm 7
    The Illusion of Routine 8
    Whispers on the Wire 9
        The View from Tripoli 11
        A Town Unaware 12
Chapter 1: A World on Edge 14
    Libya's Revolutionary Path: Gaddafi, Geopolitics, and the West 15
    The Shadow War: Covert Actions and State-Sponsored Threats 21
Chapter 2: The Routine Flight 28
    Pan Am 103 'Maid of the Seas': Passengers, Crew, and Cargo 29
    A Bomb on Board: Tracing the Unsuspected Journey 35
Chapter 4: Operation Hornbeam: Sifting the Wreckage 42
    Forging Alliances: The FBI and Dumfries Constabulary Join Forces 48
Chapter 5: The Maltese Fragment 53
    The Toshiba Bombeat: Tracing the Device 54
    Unmasking MEBO: The Zurich Connection and the Timer 58
Chapter 6: Zeroing In 63
    Intelligence Whispers: Sources and Suspicions 64
    Naming Names: The Emergence of Megrahi and Fhimah 68
Chapter 7: Standoff 74

    Indictment Issued: Justice Demanded, Justice Denied 75

    Years of Sanctions: Libya Under Pressure 80

Chapter 8: The Deal for Trial 85

    Diplomatic Breakthroughs: Mandela, Annan, and the Path to Trial 86

    A Scottish Court on Dutch Soil: Preparing the Unprecedented 91

Chapter 9: The Case for the Prosecution 96

    The Suitcase Journey: Luggage Trails and Security Lapses 97

    Star Witness: Tony Gauci and the Clothing Purchase 102

Chapter 10: The Defence Responds 106

    Attacking the Evidence: Timers, Testimony, and Doubt 107

    Alternative Theories Presented: Who Else Could Be Responsible? 113

Chapter 11: The Verdict at Camp Zeist 117

    Guilty: The Judges' Decision on Megrahi 118

    Acquitted: The Fate of Lamin Fhimah and its Implications . 123

Chapter 12: The Prisoner of Greenock 128

    Life Sentence: Inside HMP Barlinnie and Greenock 129

    Appeals and Reviews: The Fight for Exoneration Begins 133

Chapter 13: The Compassionate Release 139

    Terminal Diagnosis: The Compassionate Release Application 140

    Political Firestorm: Scotland, London, Washington, and Tripoli 145

Chapter 14: The Return and Final Years 152

    Return to Tripoli: Hero's Welcome or Quiet Decline? 153

Megrahi's Final Testimony?: Deathbed Claims and
Unanswered Calls..156

Chapter 15: Voices of the Victims..161

    Families Divided: Views on Guilt, Release, and Justice........162

    The Ongoing Campaign: Seeking Truth and Accountability.168

Chapter 16: The Enduring Lockerbie Question 173

    Beyond Megrahi?: Re-examining Evidence and Intelligence
Failures...174

    Legacy of Terror: Lessons Learned and Lessons Ignored.....180

Epilogue: Echoes in the Present...185

Prologue: The Silence Before the Storm

December 1988. The year was drawing to a close under a pall of flickering Christmas lights and the familiar hum of transatlantic commerce. Global air travel, once the domain of the affluent elite, had become an increasingly accessible conduit connecting continents, cultures, and families. Jumbo jets, symbols of technological prowess and shrinking distances, crisscrossed the skies, their cabins filled with students returning home, business travellers finalising year-end deals, soldiers heading for leave, and families anticipating reunions. The intricate dance of arrivals and departures played out daily at hubs like London Heathrow and Frankfurt Airport, monuments to movement and modernity. On the departure boards, flight numbers clicked over with reassuring regularity. Among them, Pan American World Airways Flight 103, the 'Maid of the Seas', prepared for its routine journey from London to New York's JFK, a well-trodden path across the cold North Atlantic. Few passengers settling into their seats on the Boeing 747 that evening would have felt anything other than the mundane mix of boredom and anticipation common to long-haul travel. The world, particularly the world of scheduled aviation between allied Western nations, felt knowable, manageable. This perception, however, was a fragile veneer.

The Illusion of Routine

Pan Am, despite facing financial headwinds, remained an icon. Its blue globe logo was synonymous with the 'jet age' and America's global reach. It had pioneered routes, introduced innovations, and carried generations across oceans. Flying Pan Am felt established, almost stately. The pre-flight rituals – the check-in queues, the security scan (a process far less rigorous than post-9/11 standards), the boarding calls, the safety demonstrations – were choreographed steps in a familiar ballet. Delays were an irritation, lost luggage a frustration, but the fundamental safety of the enterprise, particularly on such a flagship route between two major allied capitals, was largely taken for granted by the travelling public.

In December 1988, the rhythm of life in the United Kingdom, West Germany, and the United States pulsed with the energy of the approaching holidays. High streets bustled, carols played, and news bulletins reported on the thawing Cold War, Mikhail Gorbachev's visit to the UN, and the usual domestic political squabbles. The complexities of Middle Eastern politics or the simmering resentments harboured by states like Muammar Gaddafi's Libya seemed, for most people boarding flights like PA103, a distant, abstract backdrop – the stuff of headlines, not imminent personal danger. The sky above seemed vast and open, a realm governed by timetables and air traffic control, not by unseen plots hatched miles away. This sense of predictability, this faith in the robustness of the system, formed the bedrock of the era's travelling psychology. It was a confidence born of decades of relatively safe mass air transit, a confidence soon to be irrevocably shattered.

The very ordinariness of the day, the sheer routine of the flight's preparation, would later stand in the starkest possible contrast to the violence that awaited.

Whispers on the Wire

Yet, beneath the surface of this apparent normality, discordant notes were sounding, audible mostly within the guarded corridors of intelligence agencies and diplomatic missions. The late 1980s were not a time of global peace. State-sponsored terrorism, hijackings, and bombings were known threats, albeit often perceived as dangers concentrated in specific volatile regions. The relationship between the United States and Libya was particularly toxic. Following the 1986 US bombing raids on Tripoli and Benghazi – themselves a retaliation for the Libyan-linked bombing of the La Belle discotheque in West Berlin which killed US servicemen – tensions remained high. Libya, under the erratic and belligerent leadership of Colonel Gaddafi, was widely regarded as a pariah state, actively supporting various militant groups and implicated in numerous international incidents. More specific warnings, ambiguous yet chilling in retrospect, had surfaced. In early December, a crucial, albeit vaguely worded, communication – the so-called Helsinki warning – circulated. Originating from a purported informant, it suggested that a Pan Am flight from Frankfurt to the United States could be targeted by a bomb within a specific timeframe. The threat mentioned Abdullah, a Palestinian extremist leader, and implied the bomb might be smuggled aboard by an unwitting Finnish woman. US embassies, including those in London and Moscow, were alerted, and the warning was disseminated within aviation security circles.

However, its lack of specificity, combined with the sheer volume of threat intelligence (much of it vague or unreliable) agencies routinely handled, meant it did not trigger exceptional, publicly visible security measures on all transatlantic flights. It became one piece of data among many, its true significance tragically unrecognized until after the event.

Furthermore, the geopolitical chessboard held other potential triggers. Only five months earlier, in July 1988, the USS Vincennes, an American guided-missile cruiser operating in the Persian Gulf, had mistakenly shot down Iran Air Flight 655, killing all 290 people on board. The incident provoked outrage in Iran and across the Muslim world. While official investigations and legal proceedings would later focus squarely on Libya and its agents, the Iran Air tragedy lingered in the background, fuelling speculation about potential state-sponsored revenge, a possibility that intelligence services could not entirely dismiss in the immediate aftermath of Lockerbie, further muddying the waters. The international stage was thus primed with motives and methods, even if the specific plot targeting Flight 103 moved unseen towards its deadly conclusion. The silence was not empty; it was pregnant with unresolved conflicts and latent threats.

The View from Tripoli

Thousands of miles south, across the Mediterranean, lay the Great Socialist People's Libyan Arab Jamahiriya. Since seizing power in 1969, Muammar Gaddafi had transformed Libya from a conservative monarchy into a revolutionary state, bankrolled by oil wealth and driven by a unique blend of pan-Arabism, socialism, and Islamic theory outlined in his "Green Book." Gaddafi's Libya cultivated an image of defiance against Western imperialism and Zionism, supporting a wide array of groups, from the Irish Republican Army (IRA) to various Palestinian factions. This support often crossed the line into direct involvement in terrorism.

The nerve centre of Libya's covert operations was its intelligence apparatus, primarily the Jamahiriya Security Organization (JSO), known later as the External Security Organization (ESO). This agency was tasked with monitoring dissidents abroad, conducting espionage, and carrying out 'special operations' dictated by the regime. Within this structure worked individuals like Abdelbaset Ali Mohmed al-Megrahi. Officially, Megrahi held positions within Libyan Arab Airlines (LAA), including Head of Security, a role that granted him access to sensitive airport areas and knowledge of aviation procedures across Europe and the Middle East. His affiliation with LAA provided plausible cover for frequent travel and activities that, according to later investigations and trial evidence, were directly linked to the JSO.

While the specific orders and mechanisms behind the Lockerbie plot would be meticulously dissected in the years to come, the context of Libya in 1988 was one of a state capable of, and willing to undertake, sophisticated international operations. It possessed the motive – retaliation for the 1986 US bombings being the most cited – the means through its intelligence services and state airline, and the opportunity afforded by the security vulnerabilities of the time. The regime in Tripoli operated under its own logic, often opaque to outsiders, viewing its actions as legitimate resistance against hostile powers. From this perspective, the bustling airports of Europe were not just transit hubs, but potential arenas in a global confrontation. The planning for the storm was likely underway within this apparatus, shielded by state secrecy and the plausible deniability afforded by operating through intelligence agents under non-official cover.

A Town Unaware

Far removed from the high-stakes games of international espionage and state-sponsored terror lay the small market town of Lockerbie in Dumfries and Galloway, southwest Scotland. Nestled amidst rolling hills, it was an ordinary place known for its livestock market and quiet rural life. Its residents, numbering only a few thousand, were preparing for Christmas like families everywhere. The concerns preoccupying Lockerbie in late December 1988 were local – the weather, the festive preparations, the familiar rhythms of community life. The town existed beneath the flight paths linking Europe and North America, a geographical fact noted only by aviation enthusiasts or those occasionally glancing up at the distant contrails etching the sky.

Lockerbie was a picture of the very peace and normality that Flight 103 represented to its passengers. It was unconnected to the feuds between Washington and Tripoli, insulated from the dangers whispered about in intelligence briefings. The idea that this unassuming Scottish community could become the epicentre of Britain's deadliest terrorist attack, its name forever synonymous with a global tragedy, was utterly unthinkable. The silence here was genuine, the tranquility profound. It was the silence of lives lived far from the front lines of international conflict, soon to be violently interrupted by a horror falling, quite literally, from the sky. The storm brewing elsewhere was gathering energy, charting a course that would converge with lethal precision on this specific, unsuspecting point on the map, ensuring that Lockerbie, and the world, would never be the same. The final moments of silence were ticking away.

Chapter 1: A World on Edge

This stark declaration, delivered nearly a decade before the skies over Scotland would erupt in fire and falling debris, encapsulates the worldview that propelled Libya onto a collision course with the West. By December 1988, the name Muammar Gaddafi had become synonymous with erratic leadership, state-sponsored terrorism, and defiant anti-Western rhetoric. Understanding the tragedy of Pan Am Flight 103 requires grasping the unique trajectory of the nation Gaddafi ruled and the clandestine conflicts it waged. Libya was not merely a rogue state; it was the product of a specific revolutionary vision, vast oil wealth, and decades of escalating confrontation, creating a geopolitical powder keg long before the final, fatal spark over Lockerbie.

Libya's Revolutionary Path: Gaddafi, Geopolitics, and the West

The September Revolution and the Young Colonel

On September 1, 1969, while the aging King Idris I was abroad for medical treatment, a group of young, unknown military officers executed a swift, bloodless coup in Libya. Leading them was a charismatic, intense 27-year-old signals officer named Muammar Gaddafi. Inspired by Egypt's Gamal Abdel Nasser and the broader wave of post-colonial Arab nationalism, Gaddafi and his fellow Free Officers Movement members promised to purge Libya of foreign influence, corruption, and the perceived stagnation of the monarchy. Libya, a vast desert nation with a relatively small population, had been transformed economically by the discovery of significant oil reserves in 1959. However, under the Sanussi monarchy, much of this wealth remained concentrated, and the country hosted major Western military installations – notably Wheelus Air Base near Tripoli (a crucial US strategic facility) and British bases in Tobruk and El Adem.

Gaddafi, hailing from a Bedouin background near Sirte, possessed a fervent belief in his destiny to lead not only Libya but also the Arab world towards a new era of unity and power. He moved quickly to consolidate control, establishing the Revolutionary Command Council (RCC) as the country's supreme authority. One of the RCC's first acts was to demand the closure of the American and British military bases, a popular move that signaled a radical break from the previous regime's pro-Western alignment.

Both the US and UK, recognizing the shift in power and seeking to avoid confrontation, eventually agreed, withdrawing their forces by mid-1970. This early success bolstered Gaddafi's standing domestically and regionally, casting him as a leader unafraid to challenge the major powers.

Inventing the Jamahiriya: Ideology and Power

Gaddafi was not content merely to replace one regime with another. He sought to implement a unique political and social system, distinct from both Western liberal democracy and Soviet communism. This ambition culminated in his "Third Universal Theory," outlined in the three slim volumes of The Green Book, published between 1975 and 1979. The Green Book critiqued parliamentary democracy as a facade ("Representation is fraud") and advocated direct popular participation through a system of People's Congresses and Committees. It rejected capitalism's exploitation and communism's atheism, proposing an economic model based on worker partnerships and vague notions of Islamic socialism. In 1977, Gaddafi formally abolished the existing government structure and proclaimed the establishment of the SPLAJ – the Socialist People's Libyan Arab Jamahiriya, a neologism typically translated as "state of the masses" or "peopledom." In theory, the Jamahiriya vested power directly in the hands of the people. In practice, Gaddafi remained the ultimate authority, designated as the "Brotherly Leader and Guide of the Revolution." The intricate structure of congresses and committees often served more to control dissent and mobilize support for the regime than to facilitate genuine popular rule.

Revolutionary Committees were established as ideological watchdogs, tasked with safeguarding the revolution and suppressing opposition. This blend of populist rhetoric, Byzantine structures, and underlying authoritarian control became the hallmark of Gaddafi's Libya. His ideology, while often dismissed in the West as incoherent or bizarre, provided the justification for radical domestic policies and an assertive, often confrontational, foreign policy. He saw himself as a revolutionary thinker on par with Mao or Marx, offering a path for the Third World to escape the perceived evils of both superpowers.

Oil as a Weapon and a Tool

Libya's vast oil reserves provided Gaddafi with the financial muscle to pursue his ambitions. Soon after taking power, the RCC began demanding higher prices and greater control over production from the foreign oil companies operating in the country. Libya played a leading role within the Organization of the Petroleum Exporting Countries (OPEC) in pushing for producer nations' rights. In 1971, Libya nationalized British Petroleum's assets in retaliation for Britain's perceived role in Iran's seizure of disputed Gulf islands. This was followed by further nationalizations and forced participation agreements, effectively bringing Libya's primary source of wealth under state control by the mid-1970s.

The oil price shocks of 1973-74, partly driven by OPEC actions in which Libya was influential, dramatically increased the regime's revenues. This wealth funded significant improvements in Libyan living standards – housing, education, healthcare – solidifying Gaddafi's domestic support, particularly in the early years. However, oil revenues also became the engine for his foreign policy objectives: funding lavish diplomatic initiatives, providing aid to friendly regimes and movements across Africa and the Arab world, building up Libya's military capabilities, and, crucially, financing covert operations and support for militant groups aligned with his anti-Western, anti-imperialist agenda. Oil gave Gaddafi influence far exceeding Libya's demographic or conventional military weight, allowing him to project power and pursue ideological goals on a global scale. It transformed Libya from a sparsely populated desert kingdom into a significant, if often disruptive, player in international affairs.

Exporting Revolution: Allies and Enemies

Driven by pan-Arab ideals, Gaddafi initially sought unification with neighbouring states. Ambitious but ultimately fruitless merger attempts were made with Egypt, Sudan, Syria, and Tunisia throughout the 1970s. These failures, often resulting from Gaddafi's mercurial temperament and clashes with other Arab leaders, gradually led him to shift his focus. He increasingly positioned himself as a leader for the entire developing world, particularly Africa, championing anti-colonial struggles and supporting liberation movements financially and militarily. Groups from the Philippines (Moro National Liberation Front) to Northern Ireland (IRA) and countless factions across Africa and the Middle East received Libyan backing.

However, this support extended beyond recognized liberation movements to encompass groups widely designated as terrorist organizations. Palestinian factions, particularly radical splinter groups like Abu Nidal's Fatah-Revolutionary Council (ANO) and George Habash's Popular Front for the Liberation of Palestine (PFLP), found sanctuary, funding, and training facilities in Libya. Gaddafi saw supporting such groups as a legitimate part of the struggle against Israel and its Western backers, primarily the United States. This policy inevitably placed Libya on a collision course with Western governments. His regime became notorious for harbouring hijackers, providing arms for attacks on civilian targets, and celebrating acts of violence against perceived enemies. While Gaddafi often framed this as supporting legitimate resistance, Western capitals increasingly viewed him as a chief architect of international terrorism.

Washington Takes Notice: Escalating Confrontation

The United States initially adopted a pragmatic approach to Gaddafi's regime, prioritizing the continued flow of oil. However, relations steadily deteriorated throughout the 1970s. Libya's increasingly radical foreign policy, its support for groups targeting US interests and allies, its attempts to acquire nuclear technology, and its confrontational stance within OPEC created growing friction. The storming of the US embassy in Tripoli by protestors in 1979 (without decisive intervention by Libyan security forces) led to a suspension of US diplomatic operations.

The election of Ronald Reagan in 1981 marked a significant hardening of US policy. The Reagan administration viewed Gaddafi not just as a nuisance but as a dangerous Soviet proxy (though Libyan-Soviet relations were complex and often transactional) and a primary sponsor of global terrorism. Reagan famously labelled Gaddafi the "mad dog of the Middle East." Tensions escalated sharply in the Gulf of Sidra, which Libya claimed as territorial waters in defiance of international norms. In 1981, US Navy jets shot down two Libyan Su-22 fighters during manoeuvres in the disputed waters. Further naval exercises under Reagan's policy of challenging Libya's claim led to more confrontations. The US imposed economic sanctions, restricted travel, and actively sought to isolate Gaddafi internationally. Washington made it clear that Libyan support for terrorism would have consequences. This escalating cycle of rhetoric, sanctions, and military posturing set the stage for the direct, violent confrontations that would define US-Libyan relations in the mid-1980s, creating an atmosphere thick with animosity and the potential for explosive retaliation well before 1988. The revolutionary path Libya had embarked upon in 1969 had led it into direct, sustained conflict with the world's superpower.

The Shadow War: Covert Actions and State-Sponsored Threats

While Gaddafi's pronouncements grabbed international headlines, much of Libya's confrontation with its perceived enemies unfolded in the shadows. Clandestine operations, ranging from the assassination of political opponents to large-scale support for armed groups and direct involvement in terrorist attacks, became defining features of the Jamahiriya's foreign policy. This covert dimension, often masked by official denials and the complexities of international intelligence gathering, formed the sinister underside to Libya's revolutionary posture. By the mid-1980s, Libya was widely regarded by Western intelligence agencies as one of the world's most active and dangerous sponsors and perpetrators of state-sponsored terrorism.

Gaddafi's Eyes and Ears: The JSO

The primary instrument for Libya's covert activities was its intelligence service, known initially as the Jihaz al-Mukhabarat (General Intelligence Apparatus) and later evolving into structures like the Jamahiriya Security Organization (JSO) and eventually the External Security Organization (ESO). These agencies were responsible for both internal security – suppressing dissent against Gaddafi's rule – and external operations. They developed sophisticated capabilities in espionage, surveillance, propaganda, and, most notoriously, "special operations." Recruitment often drew from individuals loyal to Gaddafi and the principles of the revolution, sometimes operating under deep cover within Libyan embassies, state-owned enterprises like Libyan Arab Airlines (LAA), or student populations abroad.

Libyan Arab Airlines, in particular, allegedly served as a crucial logistical hub and cover for intelligence activities. Its international network provided agents with legitimate reasons for travel, access to airport facilities worldwide, and the means to transport personnel, funds, and potentially materials. Individuals like Abdelbaset al-Megrahi, holding senior positions within LAA's security apparatus while also allegedly being a ranking JSO officer, exemplified this fusion of civilian roles with clandestine intelligence functions. This dual structure provided a layer of plausible deniability for the Libyan state when its agents were implicated in illicit activities abroad. The intelligence services became Gaddafi's tool for projecting power beyond Libya's borders, enforcing loyalty, and striking at enemies, often with lethal effect.

Hunting the 'Stray Dogs'

One of the most brutal campaigns undertaken by Libyan intelligence was the systematic targeting of Libyan political dissidents living in exile. Gaddafi publicly branded these opponents – former officials, intellectuals, activists critical of his regime – as "stray dogs" and declared them legitimate targets for elimination. Starting in the late 1970s and continuing through the 1980s, a wave of assassinations and attempted assassinations shocked Libyan exile communities across Europe and the Middle East. Prominent figures were gunned down in cities like London, Rome, Bonn, Athens, and Beirut. Libyan agents, often operating with logistical support from Libyan embassies (officially known as People's Bureaus), carried out these attacks with impunity, sometimes leading to diplomatic crises. The 1980 murder of journalist Mohammad Mustafa Ramadan outside London's Regent's Park Mosque and the attempted killing of former ambassador Faisal Zagallai in Colorado in the same year were early examples. Perhaps the most infamous incident occurred in April 1984, when shots were fired from within the Libyan People's Bureau in St James's Square, London, at demonstrators protesting against Gaddafi. Woman Police Constable Yvonne Fletcher was killed, leading to an 11-day siege of the embassy and the severance of diplomatic relations between the UK and Libya. This campaign against the "stray dogs" demonstrated the ruthlessness of the Libyan regime and its willingness to commit violence on foreign soil, even against its own citizens, further cementing its pariah status.

Arming the World's Militants

Beyond targeting dissidents, Libya poured vast resources into supporting militant and terrorist organizations whose goals aligned, however loosely, with Gaddafi's anti-Western and anti-Israeli stance. This support varied widely, encompassing financial aid, military training conducted in Libyan camps, the provision of weapons and explosives, logistical assistance, and safe haven. The list of recipients was extensive and ideologically diverse. The Provisional Irish Republican Army (IRA) became a major beneficiary. Starting in the early 1970s, but escalating significantly in the mid-1980s, Libya supplied the IRA with large quantities of modern weaponry, including Semtex plastic explosive, heavy machine guns, surface-to-air missiles, and rifles. Several large shipments were intercepted, most notably the Panamanian-registered vessel Eksund seized by French authorities in 1987, carrying an estimated 150 tons of Libyan arms destined for the IRA.

The influx of Semtex, in particular, enabled the IRA to conduct a devastating bombing campaign in Northern Ireland and mainland Britain throughout the late 1980s and 1990s. Palestinian groups were also key recipients. While Gaddafi's relationship with Yasser Arafat's mainstream PLO was often fraught, more radical factions found a ready sponsor in Tripoli. The Abu Nidal Organization (ANO), notorious for its extreme violence and attacks on both Western and Arab targets, received significant backing. ANO was blamed for numerous atrocities, including the brutal synchronized attacks on Rome and Vienna airports in December 1985, which killed 20 people and injured over 100. Evidence, including forged passports used by the attackers, pointed towards Libyan complicity. Other groups, like Ahmed Jibril's Popular Front for the Liberation of Palestine-General Command (PFLP-GC), also maintained close ties with Libya, benefiting from its resources and operational latitude. This widespread support made Libya a central hub in the global network of armed militancy and terrorism.

La Belle and the Point of No Return

While support for proxies provided a degree of deniability, evidence mounted of direct Libyan involvement in terrorist attacks. The bombing of the La Belle discotheque in West Berlin on April 5, 1986, proved a pivotal moment. The nightclub, frequented by US soldiers, was devastated by a powerful explosion that killed two American servicemen and a Turkish woman, injuring over 200 others. Within days, the Reagan administration declared it had "direct, precise, and irrefutable" evidence of Libyan state involvement, citing intercepted communications between Tripoli and the Libyan

People's Bureau in East Berlin discussing the attack before and after it occurred. The intercepts reportedly indicated specific Libyan orchestration of the bombing, seemingly as retaliation for earlier US naval actions in the Gulf of Sidra. While some questions about the interpretation and completeness of the intelligence would linger, the US government presented the evidence as conclusive proof of Gaddafi's direct responsibility for murdering American citizens. For the Reagan administration, La Belle represented the crossing of a red line, demanding a forceful military response. The era of sanctions and warnings was over; direct retribution was deemed necessary.

Operation El Dorado Canyon: Retaliation and Recrimination

Ten days after the La Belle bombing, on the night of April 14-15, 1986, the United States launched Operation El Dorado Canyon, a series of coordinated air strikes against targets in Tripoli and Benghazi. US Air Force F-111 bombers flying from bases in the UK joined Navy aircraft from carriers in the Mediterranean, hitting military barracks, airfield facilities, and alleged terrorist training centres. One key target was the Bab al-Azizia compound, Gaddafi's headquarters and residence in Tripoli.

The raid was intended as a precise strike against Libya's terrorist infrastructure and leadership, designed to deter future attacks. However, inaccuracies and collateral damage resulted in civilian casualties, estimated by Libyan sources to be around 60, including the claimed death of Gaddafi's adopted infant daughter, Hanna (a claim sometimes disputed). Gaddafi himself survived, reportedly having left his residence shortly before the bombs fell.

While the Reagan administration hailed the operation as a success and a justified response to Libyan aggression, it drew condemnation from many countries, including some US allies who had refused overflight rights for the UK-based F-111s (notably France).

The long-term impact of El Dorado Canyon remains debated. Some argue it temporarily disrupted Libyan terrorist operations and forced Gaddafi to adopt a more cautious approach. Others contend it failed to eliminate the threat, potentially hardened Gaddafi's resolve, fueled anti-American sentiment, and provided Libya with a powerful motive for revenge against the United States and the United Kingdom (for facilitating the raid). From the Libyan perspective, El Dorado Canyon was an unprovoked act of state terrorism by a superpower. Whether or not it directly prompted the planning of the Lockerbie bombing nearly three years later is a central element of the enduring question, but the raid undoubtedly poisoned relations further and created a context where a devastating counter-strike became conceivable.

The Unseen Conflict Continues

Despite the shock of El Dorado Canyon, evidence suggests Libyan support for militant groups and involvement in covert plots did not cease entirely. While perhaps adopting more subtle methods, the regime's intelligence apparatus remained active. The massive arms shipments to the IRA continued into 1987. Libyan agents were still suspected in various plots and incidents across Europe and Africa. The fundamental conflict between Gaddafi's worldview and Western interests persisted.

The shadow war, marked by bombings, assassinations, arms shipments, and intelligence operations, ground on, largely invisible to the public but keenly felt within intelligence circles. It was against this backdrop of deep-seated animosity, established patterns of state-sponsored violence, and the specific grievance of the 1986 bombing raids that the events leading to December 21, 1988, unfolded. The world appeared relatively calm on the surface, but the undercurrents of conflict ran deep, dark, and dangerous.

Chapter 2: The Routine Flight

December 21, 1988. Winter solstice. As dusk settled over London, the sprawling terminals of Heathrow Airport glowed against the encroaching night. Inside Terminal 3, the air thrummed with the distinct energy of pre-Christmas travel. It was a blend of fatigue and anticipation, a cacophony of rolling suitcases, echoing announcements, and greetings in multiple languages. Tinsel garlands drooped slightly under the weight of festive expectation, strung across check-in counters and duty-free shops offering last-minute gifts. The air carried the scent of jet fuel, floor polish, and stale coffee. Outside on the damp tarmac, the vast shapes of aircraft rested between journeys, tended to by ground crews moving with practiced efficiency under the glare of floodlights. Heathrow, a critical node in the global air transport network, was operating at peak capacity, funnelling thousands of lives towards destinations across the planet. For the majority of travellers caught up in the festive rush, the journey itself was merely a means to an end – a reunion, a holiday, a return home. Among the myriad departures listed on the flickering displays, Pan American World Airways Flight 103 to New York JFK held its place, just one of many transatlantic voyages scheduled for that evening, promising arrival on the other side of the Atlantic in time for the final days before Christmas.

Pan Am 103 'Maid of the Seas': Passengers, Crew, and Cargo

The experience of checking in for an international flight in 1988 at Heathrow's Terminal 3 was a study in controlled chaos. Pan Am, despite its mounting financial difficulties, maintained a significant presence, its familiar blue globe logo a beacon for passengers navigating the terminal's lengthy corridors. Lines formed early for Flight 103, a mix of travellers reflecting the diverse currents of global mobility. Seasoned business executives stood alongside nervous first-time flyers, boisterous groups of American students returning from semesters abroad jostled good-naturedly with weary families managing children and oversized luggage. The check-in agents, working under pressure, processed passports and tickets, weighed bags often bulging with holiday purchases, and issued the flimsy, multi-part boarding passes characteristic of the era.

The questions asked were routine, focused on baggage contents mainly in the context of customs regulations and prohibited items like firearms, rather than sophisticated explosive devices. Security screening, positioned further along the path to the departure gate, involved walking through archway metal detectors – primarily effective against substantial metal objects – while hand luggage received varying degrees of attention, from a brief visual check to a pass through early-generation X-ray machines whose operators were trained mainly to spot weapons, not cleverly disguised plastic explosives. The sheer volume of passengers, combined with the imperative to maintain schedules, created an environment where thoroughness could sometimes yield to expediency.

Once checked, luggage vanished onto conveyor belts, embarking on a largely unseen journey through the airport's bowels, sorted by destination and flight number, destined for the aircraft's hold – a process reliant on efficiency but containing points of vulnerability hidden from the passengers entrusting their belongings to the system. The aircraft designated for this flight, Boeing 747-121 registration N739PA, carried the name 'Maid of the Seas'. It was an early model of the iconic Jumbo Jet, delivered to Pan Am nearly nineteen years earlier, in the pioneering days of wide-body travel. The 747 had transformed the economics and experience of flying, its immense capacity and range making intercontinental journeys accessible to millions more people. Its distinctive silhouette, dominated by the partial upper deck or 'hump', was instantly recognizable worldwide. 'Maid of the Seas' had traversed millions of miles in its service life, a veteran carrying the marks of countless journeys – minor repairs, updated avionics, the patina of age on its interior fittings.

Yet, it remained a powerful symbol of Pan Am's legacy, an airline that had once been America's unofficial flag carrier, charting routes across oceans and continents, embodying the glamour and ambition of the Jet Age. By 1988, however, Pan Am was fighting for survival. Deregulation had introduced fierce domestic competition, fuel costs had fluctuated wildly, and strategic decisions, like the sale of its invaluable Pacific routes to United Airlines in 1985, had weakened its global network. The Lockerbie disaster, when it came, would prove a blow from which the already struggling airline could never fully recover. But on this December evening, as N739PA stood at the gate, it still represented, for its crew and passengers, a reliable vessel piloted by one of the world's most experienced airlines.

Final preparations were underway: catering trucks loaded meal trays, fuel tankers pumped thousands of gallons of Jet A-1 fuel into the wing tanks, and ground engineers completed their walk-around checks. A significant portion of the passengers joining Flight 103 at Heathrow had begun their journey elsewhere. Pan Am Flight 103A, operated by a smaller Boeing 727, served as a crucial feeder flight, originating that morning in Berlin, stopping in Frankfurt, and then flying on to London. Frankfurt Airport, a major continental European hub, was the collection point for passengers from various parts of Germany and beyond. The 727 arrived at Heathrow carrying not just connecting passengers but also their checked baggage, which needed to be transferred to the waiting 747.

This interlining process was standard operating procedure for hub-and-spoke airline networks, maximizing efficiency by channelling passengers from multiple origins onto larger aircraft for the main leg of the journey. Passengers from PA103A, identifiable by their Pan Am boarding passes and luggage tags indicating the final destination JFK, disembarked and made their way through the labyrinthine corridors of Terminal 3, following signs for flight connections towards the gate where the 'Maid of the Seas' awaited. Their luggage, unloaded from the 727's hold, was placed onto baggage carts for the short journey across the tarmac to be sorted and loaded onto the 747. This transfer point, occurring under time pressure and involving coordination between different ground crews and baggage systems, represented a critical juncture, particularly for any piece of luggage whose journey had originated before Frankfurt.

The seamless flow of interline baggage, essential for airline operations, relied on assumptions about the integrity of bags entering the system at earlier points – assumptions that, on this day, proved fatally flawed. Ensuring the safety and smooth operation of the flight deck were three highly experienced aviators. Captain Jim MacQuarrie, residing in New Hampshire, brought the quiet confidence born of decades spent flying complex aircraft across vast distances. His extensive record on the 747 made him intimately familiar with the aircraft's systems and handling characteristics. First Officer Ray Wagner, from New Jersey, possessed a similarly impressive logbook, complementing the captain's experience. Flight Engineer Jerry Avritt, based near New York City, was responsible for monitoring the intricate mechanical and electronic systems of the 747, managing fuel consumption, electrical power, hydraulics, and pressurization – a vital role on these older-generation Jumbos which required a three-person flight crew.

Their combined expertise represented thousands upon thousands of hours of safe operation, a testament to the rigorous training and professionalism demanded by international airlines. As they went through their pre-flight checks, consulting weather reports, confirming fuel loads, and programming the flight management systems, their actions were precise, methodical, honed by years of repetition. In the main cabin, Purser Mary Murphy led a team of thirteen flight attendants responsible for the well-being of the 243 passengers. The cabin crew, a diverse group reflecting Pan Am's global workforce, prepared the aircraft for boarding, checking emergency equipment – oxygen masks, life vests, evacuation slides – ensuring galleys were stocked for the transatlantic service, and coordinating with the ground staff.

As passengers began to board, the flight attendants directed them to their seats, assisted with stowing cabin baggage, and offered welcoming smiles, projecting an air of calm competence. Their role extended far beyond serving drinks and meals; they were the first line of response in any onboard emergency, trained to manage everything from medical incidents to security threats and, in the worst-case scenario, aircraft evacuations. They moved through the aisles, securing overhead bins and ensuring passengers were settled, their familiar routines part of the ritual designed to make air travel feel safe and ordinary.

The passenger manifest for Pan Am 103 read like a roll call of late 20th-century global society. The overwhelming majority were Americans, nearly 190 souls heading towards the United States just days before Christmas. Among them, the largest single group comprised the 35 students from Syracuse University, their youthful energy infectious. They were returning from study programmes in London and Florence, their minds filled with memories of European adventures, their bags likely stuffed with souvenirs and laundry. They represented the bright promise of education and international exchange, a promise tragically unfulfilled. Families were also prominent: parents travelling to join children, children going to visit grandparents, entire family units embarking on holiday trips. The emotional weight of these festive journeys, the anticipation of reunions, added a particular poignancy in retrospect. Business travellers occupied many seats, executives from multinational corporations like Volkswagen, engineers, consultants, individuals whose work routinely took them across continents.

The flight also carried personnel linked to the US government and military, including Matthew Gannon, the CIA's deputy station chief in Beirut, whose presence fuelled persistent, though unproven, theories about targeted assassination motives behind the bombing. Adding to the international mix were citizens from 20 other countries. Bernt Carlsson, the UN Commissioner for Namibia, was perhaps the most prominent non-American victim, a seasoned diplomat on a mission of peace, heading to New York for the signing of accords that would finally grant independence to the territory he oversaw. His death represented a stark collision between the painstaking work of international diplomacy and the brutal calculus of terrorism. Passengers represented a spectrum of ages, backgrounds, and purposes – academics, artists, tourists, retirees. Each boarded the 'Maid of the Seas' with their own individual narrative, their own reason for making the journey that night, unknowingly converging towards a single, violent destiny dictated by forces far beyond their control.

While passengers settled into their seats, the final stages of loading were completed below deck. The Boeing 747's underbelly contains vast cargo holds capable of swallowing tons of luggage, mail, and commercial freight, packed into dozens of aluminium Unit Load Devices (ULDs). These standardized containers, shaped to fit snugly within the aircraft's contours, are essential for efficient loading and unloading. Ground crews, working against the clock to maintain the schedule, used specialized loaders to lift the heavy containers into the forward and aft holds. Each container's position is carefully recorded as part of the aircraft's weight and balance calculations, critical for ensuring aerodynamic stability during flight.

Container AVE 4041 PA, containing bags transferred from the feeder flight PA103A arriving from Frankfurt, was manoeuvered into position 14L in the forward cargo hold. This location was relatively close to the outer skin of the aircraft on the port (left) side, just ahead of the massive wing box structure that forms the junction between the wings and the fuselage. Within this container, amidst the jumble of ordinary suitcases filled with clothes, toiletries, and Christmas gifts, lay the Samsonite Silhouette 4000 suitcase, indistinguishable from the outside but carrying within it the means of the aircraft's destruction. Once loading was complete, the heavy cargo doors were swung shut and locked, securing the hold. The final walk-around check was completed, ground service vehicles pulled away, and the flight crew received their clearance for pushback.

A Bomb on Board: Tracing the Unsuspected Journey

The catastrophic failure that allowed an explosive device to be loaded onto Pan Am Flight 103 stemmed from critical weaknesses in the aviation security systems prevalent in 1988. These systems relied on a patchwork of measures that, while intended to deter or detect threats, contained exploitable gaps. Passenger screening, typically involving walk-through metal detectors, was primarily designed against hijackings using firearms or large knives, not against sophisticated bombs built with non-metallic or disguised components. X-ray technology for carry-on bags was rudimentary compared to modern multi-view and trace-detection systems. Crucially, the screening of checked baggage was inconsistent and technologically limited. While some airports, including Frankfurt and Heathrow, did employ X-ray machines for checked luggage, these were *often deployed selectively (e.g., focusing on specific routes or passenger profiles deemed higher risk) and their ability to reliably detect plastic explosives cleverly concealed within electronic devices was minimal. Operators were often looking for the tell-tale shapes of guns or grenades, not amorphous slabs of Semtex moulded to fit inside a radio. A more significant procedural defence was supposed to be passenger-baggage reconciliation. International Civil Aviation Organization (ICAO) guidelines recommended that airlines ensure every piece of checked luggage loaded onto an international flight belonged to a passenger who had actually boarded that same flight. This principle aimed specifically to prevent the scenario of an unaccompanied bag containing a bomb being loaded by terrorists who had no intention of travelling themselves.*

However, the implementation of baggage reconciliation in 1988 was fraught with difficulties. Procedures were often manual, involving cross-checking baggage tag numbers against passenger manifests – a cumbersome process prone to error, especially under time pressure. More critically, the rules and their enforcement varied significantly between airlines and airports, and there were often specific exemptions or less stringent procedures applied to interline baggage – bags transferred from another airline or flight. The complexity of tracking a bag that might have passed through multiple airports and airline systems before reaching its final flight created loopholes. It was precisely this vulnerability, the potential for an unaccompanied interline bag to slip through the net, that the perpetrators of the Lockerbie bombing targeted with lethal precision. Previous incidents, such as the 1985 bombing of Air India Flight 182 which was also traced to an unaccompanied bag originating from a connecting flight, had tragically highlighted these weaknesses, yet comprehensive, globally enforced reforms had not yet been implemented. The intricate forensic investigation following the destruction of Pan Am 103 pointed investigators towards an origin far from Heathrow or Frankfurt. Debris analysis revealed that the explosion originated within the forward cargo hold, specifically within container AVE 4041 PA which held bags transferred from the Frankfurt feeder flight. Microscopic fragments of material embedded within the wreckage were painstakingly identified. Some came from a specific type of bronze-coloured Samsonite Silhouette 4000 suitcase. Others were fibres from clothing – slacks, a cardigan, a baby-gro – traced through manufacturing records and diligent detective work to a single shop, Mary's House, in Sliema, Malta. The owner of Mary's House, Tony Gauci, provided investigators with a crucial, though later contested, eyewitness account. He recalled selling these specific items of clothing in late November or early December 1988 to a man he described as Libyan, whom he later, under complex circumstances including seeing him on television after his indictment, identified as Abdelbaset al-Megrahi. This clothing evidence formed a key pillar of the prosecution's case linking the bomb bag to Malta and, allegedly, to Megrahi.

Further strengthening the Malta connection was the discovery of a tiny fragment, no bigger than a fingernail, of printed circuit board. This fragment, recovered from a piece of wreckage miles from Lockerbie, was identified by intelligence analysts and electronics experts as part of an MST-13 digital timer. The manufacturer, MEBO AG of Zurich, Switzerland, confirmed that this specific type of sophisticated timer, capable of precise detonation timing, had been manufactured exclusively for, and supplied only to, the Libyan military and intelligence services.

This timer fragment became the critical piece of forensic evidence suggesting not only that the bomb originated outside the UK, but also pointing directly towards Libyan involvement. Based on this evidence trail – the clothing purchased in Malta, the timer linked to Libya, the bomb container holding bags from Frankfurt – investigators constructed the narrative that the bomb was assembled in Malta. It was likely placed inside the Samsonite suitcase, surrounded by the newly purchased clothes to aid concealment and perhaps add legitimacy if the bag were opened, and then introduced into the baggage system at Malta's Luqa Airport on the morning of December 21st, tagged for Pan Am Flight 103 via Frankfurt and London. The linchpin of this theory was that the suitcase travelled as unaccompanied baggage on Air Malta Flight KM180 from Luqa to Frankfurt, exploiting lax reconciliation procedures for interline transfers.

Upon arrival at Frankfurt Airport, the baggage from Air Malta KM180, including the unaccompanied Samsonite, entered the complex ecosystem of one of Europe's primary aviation crossroads. Frankfurt handled enormous volumes of transfer traffic, with bags moving between dozens of airlines and connecting flights. The unaccompanied suitcase, tagged for PA103 to JFK, needed to be transferred to the Pan Am system for loading onto the feeder flight, PA103A. Investigations into Pan Am's operations at Frankfurt revealed potential security gaps during this critical transfer window. While Pan Am had procedures for screening originating baggage, the protocols for screening interline bags arriving from other carriers were less clear and possibly not rigorously applied, especially given the sheer volume and time constraints.

There was no definitive record confirming that the specific baggage container holding the suspect suitcase was X-rayed at Frankfurt before being loaded onto the Boeing 727 bound for Heathrow. Furthermore, effective passenger-baggage reconciliation for these transit bags appears to have been absent. The unaccompanied bag, therefore, successfully navigated the Frankfurt transfer, blending in with legitimate luggage, its deadly nature undetected. It was loaded onto PA103A, taking the next step closer to its target.

The final transfer occurred at Heathrow, arguably the point of greatest vulnerability within the Pan Am system itself. When PA103A arrived from Frankfurt, its baggage was unloaded and moved across the tarmac to where the 'Maid of the Seas' was being prepared. The bags from Frankfurt, including the Samsonite, were mixed with the much larger volume of luggage checked in directly by passengers boarding at Heathrow. These bags were then sorted and loaded into the ULD containers destined for the 747's hold. Container AVE 4041 PA received bags from the Frankfurt flight. Once again, the investigation concluded that robust passenger-baggage reconciliation procedures were not effectively applied to the interline bags arriving from Frankfurt before they were loaded onto the main flight, PA103. The focus was on ensuring all locally checked bags were accounted for and that the aircraft departed on time. The unaccompanied bag, having already passed through Malta and Frankfurt without being intercepted or reconciled against a boarding passenger, successfully completed its journey into the forward cargo hold of the 'Maid of the Seas'. It was placed inside container AVE 4041 PA, which was then mechanically hoisted and locked into position 14L.

The device itself was a testament to the deadly ingenuity of bomb-makers aiming to circumvent contemporary security measures. The core charge consisted of Semtex-H, a powerful plastic explosive manufactured in Czechoslovakia and known to be in Libyan inventory. Semtex is stable, putty-like, and difficult to detect by the simple metal detectors or early X-ray machines of the era. Its malleability allowed it to be moulded into the casing of a Toshiba RT-SF16 'Bombeat' radio cassette player, a popular and unremarkable consumer electronic device. Hollowing out the radio and filling the space with Semtex disguised the explosive mass, making it appear as innocuous components on an X-ray image. The triggering mechanism was the sophisticated Swiss-made MST-13 electronic timer, chosen for its reliability and precision over cruder barometric fuses (which trigger based on altitude) or simple acid-delay timers. This allowed the perpetrators to set a specific time interval for detonation, calculated to occur well into the flight, likely over the ocean or at cruising altitude where the atmospheric pressure difference and aerodynamic forces would maximize the aircraft's disintegration upon explosion. Powered by batteries concealed within the radio, the timer, once activated, began its silent countdown.

The entire assembly, nested within the Samsonite suitcase and surrounded by clothing, represented a lethal package engineered to appear ordinary while delivering catastrophic destructive power at a predetermined moment. At 6:04 PM GMT, Pan Am Flight 103, slightly behind schedule, was pushed back from the gate at Heathrow Terminal 3. The four massive Pratt & Whitney JT9D engines spooled up with a rising whine. Captain MacQuarrie taxied the heavy aircraft towards Runway 27R.

Following final clearance from air traffic control, at 6:25 PM, the brakes were released, and the 'Maid of the Seas' accelerated down the runway, lifting gracefully into the cold, dark sky. It climbed steadily, banking towards the northwest, following the standard departure route that would take it over the English Midlands. On the flight deck, the crew retracted the flaps and landing gear, engaged the autopilot, and communicated with air traffic controllers, receiving instructions for their climb towards the designated cruising altitude of 31,000 feet. In the cabin, the lights were adjusted, and the flight attendants began preparations for the evening meal service. Passengers settled in, anticipating the routine six-hour flight ahead. The aircraft crossed the coast near the Solway Firth, entering Scottish airspace as it continued its climb. Below, the scattered lights of towns and villages passed by unnoticed. Inside the forward cargo hold, amidst the darkness and the vibrating hum of the engines, the hidden timer continued its inexorable progression, second by second, towards detonation. The routine flight was proceeding exactly as planned, utterly unaware of the precise, calculated violence counting down in its heart.

Chapter 4: Operation Hornbeam: Sifting the Wreckage

The dawn of December 22nd, 1988, cast a cold, revealing light over the wreckage-strewn landscape of Lockerbie and its environs. The immediate, instinctive response of rescue, driven by the desperate hope of finding survivors, had tragically given way overnight to the stark realization that this was now a recovery operation on an unprecedented scale. The intense orange glow of the fires that had dominated the night sky, particularly the inferno consuming Sherwood Crescent, had subsided into smouldering ruins emitting plumes of acrid smoke into the still morning air. As the true extent of the devastation became visible – the fragmentation of the giant aircraft, the vast dispersal of its contents, the catastrophic impact on the town – the focus shifted irrevocably. What had begun as a local emergency response transformed into arguably the most complex crime scene investigation ever initiated on British soil. For the officers of Dumfries and Galloway Constabulary and the multitude of assisting agencies converging on this small corner of Scotland, the challenge was immense: to meticulously gather the fragments of evidence, recover the victims with dignity, and begin the painstaking process of understanding how and why Pan Am Flight 103 fell from the sky.

Scotland's Largest Crime Scene: The Grim Task of Recovery

The legal and practical complexities began with the sheer scale of the area involved. Dumfries and Galloway Constabulary, under the leadership of Chief Constable John Orr – a man suddenly thrust from managing regional policing concerns into coordinating a global incident – took the necessary step of declaring an enormous swathe of territory an official crime scene. This area ultimately encompassed some 845 square miles, reflecting the horrifying reality that the Boeing 747 had disintegrated at high altitude, scattering its contents over vast distances. The designated zone stretched from Lockerbie itself eastward, following the prevailing winds on the night, across farmland, through dense Forestry Commission plantations like the Eskdalemuir Forest, over rolling hills and moorland, extending towards the English border near Newcastleton and even reaching the North Sea coast where lighter debris was later found washed ashore. Securing such a vast, complex, and largely rural area was a task of Herculean proportions.

It involved establishing cordons around key impact sites within Lockerbie, controlling access points on rural roads, and initiating systematic searches across terrain that varied from residential streets and gardens to remote, boggy uplands and densely wooded areas. Maintaining the integrity of potential evidence scattered across this huge expanse, while also managing the necessary activities of emergency services, recovery teams, and eventually, the returning lives of local residents, required constant vigilance and meticulous planning.

The official police investigation received its operational designation: Operation Hornbeam. The name, drawn sequentially from a predetermined list, would become synonymous with the years of painstaking detective work that followed. Its initial objectives, however, were rooted in the immediate aftermath. The first, and most sensitive, priority was the location and recovery of all 270 victims – the 11 residents killed in Sherwood Crescent and the 259 passengers and crew members whose bodies lay scattered across the crime scene. This demanded a systematic approach. Detailed maps of the entire 845-square-mile area were divided into zones, which were further subdivided into smaller, manageable grids.

Search teams, often comprising lines of police officers and soldiers moving slowly across the terrain, were assigned specific grids each day. Their task was methodical and harrowing: to visually scan every square metre of ground, looking for human remains, items of wreckage, or personal property. Given the nature of the aircraft's disintegration and impact, remains were often fragmented and widely dispersed, requiring intense concentration and emotional resilience from the searchers. Protocols dictated that upon finding suspected human remains, the search line would halt, the location would be precisely marked and recorded, and specialist forensic recovery teams would be called in to handle the remains with care and dignity, ensuring proper evidence handling procedures were followed. The physical demands were immense, involving long hours of walking across uneven, often muddy or frozen ground, frequently in adverse winter weather conditions – rain, sleet, snow, and biting winds swept across the Scottish border region in the days and weeks following the disaster.

The psychological toll on the searchers, many of whom were young police constables or soldiers facing such horror for the first time, was profound. They were confronted daily with scenes of unimaginable trauma, discovering not only victims but also poignant personal items – photographs, letters, children's toys – that underscored the human tragedy. Support systems, including counselling services, were eventually put in place, but the immediate burden fell heavily on the individuals and their team leaders. The recovery effort drew personnel from across the UK: hundreds of police officers seconded from forces in Scotland, England, and Wales worked alongside soldiers primarily from the 1st Battalion, King's Own Scottish Borderers (KOSB), whose barracks were relatively nearby and whose personnel possessed invaluable local knowledge and discipline. Specialist teams, including Scottish Mountain Rescue volunteers accustomed to searching remote areas, and Royal Air Force search and rescue teams with helicopters, played crucial roles, particularly in accessing difficult terrain. The temporary mortuary facilities became centres of quiet, intense activity. Lockerbie Academy's gymnasium was transformed, lined with refrigerated containers, examination tables, and X-ray equipment. Pathologists, forensic dentists, fingerprint experts, and DVI specialists from the UK and abroad worked relentlessly to identify the victims, meticulously comparing post-mortem findings with ante-mortem records – dental charts, medical X-rays, fingerprints, DNA samples (though DNA technology was less advanced than today), and descriptions provided by heartbroken families who travelled to Lockerbie from around the world, facing the agonizing process of providing information and awaiting confirmation.

Parallel to the victim recovery was the equally critical task of retrieving the aircraft wreckage, led by investigators from the Air Accidents Investigation Branch (AAIB). Arriving within hours of the crash, the AAIB team brought specialist knowledge of aircraft structures, systems, and failure analysis. Their initial priority was locating the flight recorders. The Cockpit Voice Recorder (CVR), capturing the final conversations on the flight deck, and the Flight Data Recorder (FDR), logging hundreds of parameters about the aircraft's performance, were crucial. Using specialized locator beacons and detailed analysis of the debris trail, both recorders were found within the first 24-48 hours – a significant early success for the investigation. The FDR confirmed the aircraft was operating normally until the moment of the event; the CVR tragically captured only a sudden, unidentified noise just before cutting out, indicating the speed and violence of the initial explosion near the flight deck.

Beyond the recorders, the AAIB coordinated the mapping and recovery of the entire aircraft structure. This involved identifying every significant piece of wreckage, from the largest sections – engines, landing gear, fuselage segments, tailplane – down to smaller fragments. The location of each piece was precisely plotted on maps. This debris distribution analysis was vital: the pattern showed that lighter pieces from the forward fuselage had travelled furthest east, confirming that the initial catastrophic event occurred near the front of the aircraft. Heavier components, like the engines and wing box, followed a more ballistic trajectory, explaining their impact closer to Lockerbie town. This painstaking mapping allowed investigators to pinpoint the likely area within the aircraft where the disintegration began.

Collecting the wreckage required a major logistical operation, involving cranes, low-loaders, helicopters for inaccessible items, and thousands of evidence bags for smaller pieces. Every recovered item was tagged, photographed in situ, and transported to a secure Royal Air Force maintenance hangar at Longtown, near Carlisle. Inside this vast space, AAIB investigators, assisted by engineers from Boeing and engine manufacturers Pratt & Whitney, began the monumental task of laying out the recovered wreckage in a rough approximation of the original aircraft structure. This allowed them to examine fracture surfaces, deformation patterns, and look for the telltale micro-physical evidence of an explosion – pitting, cratering, soot deposits, and chemical residues – that would differentiate bomb damage from simple structural failure due to aerodynamic overload.

A third stream of recovery focused on personal belongings. The contents of dozens of suitcases, along with items from the passenger cabin, were scattered across the landscape. Operation Hornbeam personnel undertook the emotionally taxing work of collecting these items. Wallets containing final family photographs, diaries detailing recent European travels, unopened Christmas presents, business documents, university textbooks – each discovery was a poignant reminder of the individual lives extinguished. These items were carefully logged and stored, both for potential forensic value (especially luggage fragments found near the blast epicentre) and with the eventual aim of returning identifiable property to bereaved families, a process that would take months and years. The sheer quantity of material recovered – human remains, aircraft wreckage measured in tons, thousands of personal items – required the establishment of robust evidence management systems from the outset.

Maintaining the chain of custody for every item, ensuring accurate labelling and storage, and creating comprehensive databases were essential for the integrity of both the air accident investigation and the criminal inquiry. The fields, forests, and streets around Lockerbie became the site of an unprecedented forensic harvest, conducted under immense pressure and scrutiny, forming the foundation upon which the subsequent investigations would be built.

Forging Alliances: The FBI and Dumfries Constabulary Join Forces

The strong suspicion, hardening almost immediately into certainty, that Pan Am 103 was brought down by a terrorist bomb fundamentally changed the nature of the investigation. While the AAIB focused on the technical 'what' and 'how' of the aircraft's destruction for safety purposes, the imperative shifted towards discovering the 'who' and 'why' – a criminal investigation targeting mass murder. Given the aircraft's American registration and the staggering loss of American life (189 citizens), the involvement of the United States government and the FBI was not just anticipated but legally mandated under statutes covering terrorist acts against US nationals and interests overseas. This set the stage for an unprecedented partnership between the lead investigating authority, the relatively small Dumfries and Galloway Constabulary operating within the distinct Scottish legal system, and the powerful resources of a global superpower's premier law enforcement agency.

Within a day of the disaster, FBI personnel began arriving in Lockerbie. Initial contact was made through the Bureau's Legal Attaché office in London, paving the way for senior investigators and forensic experts to deploy from the US. The potential for jurisdictional conflict was significant. The crime had occurred in Scotland, meaning any future prosecution would take place in a Scottish court, under Scottish law, directed by the independent Crown Office and Procurator Fiscal Service (COPFS), headed by the Lord Advocate. Dumfries and Galloway Constabulary held territorial responsibility for the investigation on the ground. Yet, the FBI had a clear legal mandate to investigate the deaths of its citizens and possessed resources and international reach far exceeding those of the Scottish police. Overcoming these potential divisions required immediate efforts to build trust and establish clear working protocols. Chief Constable John Orr proved instrumental, displaying leadership that balanced the needs of the Scottish investigation with the necessity of close collaboration with the Americans. Senior FBI officials, recognizing the sensitivity of operating on foreign soil and the expertise of the Scottish investigators, reciprocal showed respect for Scottish primacy while making their resources available.

A framework for joint operation was rapidly established. It was agreed that while the Scottish police maintained lead responsibility within the UK, the FBI would be fully integrated into the investigation structure. Joint teams were formed for key functions like evidence collection, witness interviews, and intelligence analysis. A major incident complex was set up, initially based in Lockerbie High School and police stations, later expanding to facilities in Carlisle, providing shared office space, communication links, and evidence management systems accessible to both Scottish police and FBI personnel. Crucially, protocols for evidence handling were meticulously developed to satisfy both jurisdictions. Procedures for documenting the chain of custody, conducting forensic examinations (with analysis potentially occurring in UK Home Office labs, Scottish police labs, and the FBI Laboratory in Quantico, Virginia), and sharing results had to be robust enough to withstand scrutiny in both Scottish and potentially US courts. This required legal experts from both sides – Scottish Procurators Fiscal and FBI lawyers – to work closely together from the earliest stages. The level of integration achieved, with FBI agents working alongside Scottish detectives in incident rooms and conducting joint interviews, was groundbreaking for its time and largely successful due to the shared determination of the individuals involved.

The investigation proceeded along two parallel tracks: the AAIB's technical inquiry and the joint police/FBI criminal probe, though the lines often blurred in practice. The AAIB's findings about the location and nature of the explosion, derived from detailed wreckage analysis and flight recorder data, were critical feeds into the criminal investigation. Once the AAIB confirmed evidence of a high-explosive detonation originating in container AVE 4041 PA, the criminal teams could focus their forensic efforts intensely on debris recovered from that specific container and its position in the forward cargo hold. The police and FBI, meanwhile, focused on the human element: who could have placed the bomb? How did it get onto the aircraft? They began the laborious process of tracing the provenance of every piece of luggage loaded onto PA103 and its feeder flight PA103A. Passenger manifests were analyzed, background checks run.

Witness interviews extended beyond Lockerbie residents to include airport workers at Heathrow, Frankfurt, and eventually Malta, as leads began to emerge. The investigation rapidly expanded internationally, requiring formal requests for assistance through diplomatic and legal channels to authorities in Germany, Malta, Switzerland (regarding the timer manufacturer MEBO), and numerous other countries implicated through passenger movements or intelligence leads.

The complementary strengths of the partner agencies became apparent. Dumfries and Galloway Constabulary provided intimate local knowledge, dedicated officers experienced in traditional detective work, and the legal authority to operate within Scotland. The FBI brought immense resources: hundreds of agents available for deployment globally, advanced forensic capabilities at their Quantico laboratory (particularly in explosive residue analysis and electronics), sophisticated intelligence analysis tools, and established relationships with law enforcement agencies worldwide, facilitating international inquiries. The Procurator Fiscal service provided essential legal guidance, ensuring the investigation complied with Scottish evidence rules and procedures, crucial for any future prosecution. Additionally, intelligence agencies in both the UK (MI5, MI6) and the US (CIA) played vital background roles, sharing relevant intelligence assessments about terrorist groups, state sponsors, and potential threats, although maintaining the necessary separation between intelligence information and admissible evidence remained a constant consideration for the criminal investigators.

The sheer volume of information generated – witness statements, forensic reports, intelligence logs, recovered documents, evidence inventories – required powerful computer databases (relatively new technology for such large-scale investigations in 1988) to manage and cross-reference effectively. Operation Hornbeam, born from tragedy in a small Scottish town, quickly evolved into a complex, globe-spanning investigation, powered by an unprecedented alliance determined to unravel the conspiracy behind the bombing and bring those responsible to justice. The path ahead would be long and arduous, but the foundations for the hunt were firmly laid in those demanding early days amidst the wreckage.

Chapter 5: The Maltese Fragment

In the cold, echoing expanse of the RAF hangar at Longtown, a unique and sombre form of archaeology was underway. Spread across the vast concrete floor lay the dismembered corpse of Pan Am Flight 103. Investigators moved with quiet intensity through this landscape of twisted aluminium, shattered composites, and severed wires, engaged in a task both monumental and microscopic: coaxing secrets from the wreckage.

The sheer scale was overwhelming – acres of debris representing almost the entirety of a Boeing 747, painstakingly recovered from the 845 square miles of Scottish countryside designated as Operation Hornbeam's primary search area. Each piece, from multi-ton engine pods down to rivet heads and plastic shards, was meticulously tagged, logged, and positioned in a rough three-dimensional layout corresponding to its original place on the aircraft. It was within this metallic graveyard, under the harsh fluorescent lights and the constant pressure of a global investigation, that the critical forensic breakthroughs would occur – discoveries reliant on advanced science, international cooperation, and an almost obsessive attention to the smallest fragments of evidence, fragments that would ultimately point the finger towards a Mediterranean island and a shadowy Swiss electronics firm.

The Toshiba Bombeat: Tracing the Device

The initial forensic thrust, conducted jointly by the AAIB's technical experts and specialist forensic scientists supporting the police investigation, focused on confirming the suspicion of an explosion and locating its precise origin. This involved laborious examination of thousands of pieces of wreckage retrieved from the forward cargo hold area, identified through the debris plot as the likely source of the initial disintegration. Investigators scrutinized fractured metal surfaces under magnification, looking for the characteristic signs of explosive damage: the microscopic pitting and cratering caused by the immense, instantaneous pressure of a high-explosive detonation impacting metal; the outward 'petalling' of torn fuselage skin, indicating force emanating from within; specific types of heat damage and soot deposition inconsistent with a simple fuel fire. Chemical swabs were taken from suspect surfaces and analyzed using techniques like gas chromatography-mass spectrometry, searching for the residual trace molecules of specific explosive compounds.

This meticulous work, carried out over weeks and months, confirmed the presence of residues characteristic of PETN and RDX, the primary components of Semtex plastic explosive. Furthermore, the damage patterns converged overwhelmingly on one specific area: the cluster of wreckage associated with Unit Load Device AVE 4041 PA, a baggage container loaded at Heathrow with luggage transferred from the Pan Am feeder flight originating in Frankfurt. Within the debris mapped to this container, the damage analysis pointed even more precisely to a single piece of luggage as the seat of the explosion.

Identifying that specific piece of luggage amidst the shredded remains of potentially hundreds of bags within AVE 4041 PA was another immense challenge. Investigators painstakingly collected and sorted fragments of suitcases – fabric, leather, plastic mouldings, metal fittings. They began to identify pieces exhibiting the most severe explosive damage, indicating proximity to the blast centre. Among these, multiple fragments were matched, based on colour, texture, and material composition, to a particular model of suitcase: a bronze-coloured, hard-sided Samsonite Silhouette 4000. While a popular brand, knowing the specific model provided investigators with crucial details about its construction and materials. But the suitcase itself was merely the outer vessel.

The real breakthrough came with the discovery of numerous small, non-aircraft related fragments found intimately associated with the most heavily damaged Samsonite pieces – shards of dark plastic, pieces of electronic circuit board, speaker grille fragments, and components like capacitors and resistors. These items immediately raised flags. Forensic teams, drawing on expertise in electronics and consumer products, began the complex task of identifying these fragments. They compared shapes, mouldings, component types, and circuit board layouts against technical specifications and exemplar models of thousands of electronic devices manufactured in the 1980s. Through this meticulous comparative analysis, they achieved a positive identification: the fragments belonged to a Toshiba Model RT-SF16 radio cassette player, a popular portable stereo often marketed under the name 'Bombeat'. Its relatively common availability perhaps made it an ideal choice for concealment, unlikely to attract undue attention.

The identification of the Toshiba Bombeat provided a clear hypothesis for the bomb's construction. Investigators theorized that the perpetrators had removed the radio's internal components – potentially the bulky speaker magnets, transformer, and cassette mechanism – creating a void within the plastic casing. This space would then have been packed with plastic explosive, likely Semtex given the residues found. The explosive could be moulded to fit the available space, perhaps leaving some original electronic components visible near the surface or repositioning them to enhance the disguise. The Semtex, being dense and putty-like, could be packed tightly, achieving a significant explosive charge (estimated eventually at 340-450 grams) within a relatively small volume. The radio's casing then served as the perfect Trojan horse, concealing the lethal contents within an object that might appear relatively unremarkable on the baggage X-ray systems of 1988, which were primarily designed to detect the characteristic shapes of metallic weapons rather than amorphous blocks of plastic explosive hidden within electronics.

Yet, perhaps the most astonishing forensic discovery related to the bomb suitcase came from the realm of textile analysis. Embedded deep within the fibres of the shattered Samsonite fragments, fused by the heat and force of the blast to remnants of the Toshiba radio casing, investigators found minuscule scraps of clothing. Recovering these fragile fibres without causing further damage required extreme care. Forensic scientists, working under microscopes, used specialized tools to separate these textile fragments from the surrounding debris. Each fibre was then subjected to a battery of sophisticated analytical techniques. Polarized light microscopy revealed the fibre types – wool, cotton, acrylics.

Microspectrophotometry analyzed the specific dyes used, creating a unique colour profile. Comparison with extensive databases of clothing manufacturers allowed the scientists to identify the garments from which these tiny fragments originated with remarkable specificity. They determined the fibres came from several distinct items: a man's tweed jacket (specifically identified as Yorkie brand), a brown acrylic herringbone-patterned cardigan (C&A brand), grey flannel trousers (Levi Strauss), blue pyjamas, and, incongruously, a white cotton baby-gro (Babygro brand, size 3-6 months).

This precise identification of multiple specific clothing items, all apparently packed within the primary bomb suitcase, presented investigators with a powerful new lead. Tracing the retail distribution of these specific brands and models was a complex task involving international inquiries with manufacturers and retailers. Months of painstaking work eventually led to a single, exclusive point of sale for this particular combination of garments: Mary's House, a clothing boutique located in the town of Sliema, on the island of Malta. The statistical probability of these specific items, originating from different manufacturers but sold together through one small shop in Malta, ending up by chance in the suitcase that exploded over Lockerbie was deemed vanishingly small. This forensic link was concrete and compelling. Investigators from Operation Hornbeam, including Scottish detectives and FBI agents, travelled to Malta in early 1989. They interviewed the shop owner, Tony Gauci, presenting him with information about the clothing items. Gauci confirmed selling such items and, based on his recollection of a specific, unusual sale involving this combination of menswear and a baby-gro, provided a description of the purchaser – a man he believed was Libyan, who paid in cash, and seemed indifferent to the sizes.

He also recalled selling the man an umbrella during the transaction, potentially helping to date the purchase to a rainy day in late November or early December 1988. While the full complexities of Gauci's testimony and his later controversial identification of Megrahi would unfold over time, this initial forensic connection between the clothing packed around the bomb and a specific point of purchase in Malta provided the investigation with its first major geographical anchor outside of the UK and Germany. The 'Maltese fragment' was no longer just a piece of timer; it was now also woven into the very fabric of the clothes that had surrounded the bomb.

Unmasking MEBO: The Zurich Connection and the Timer

While the investigation into the bomb's container and contents progressed, another team of forensic specialists focused intensely on identifying the detonation mechanism. If the Toshiba radio was the body, and the Semtex the muscle, the timer was the brain. Locating remnants of such a device amidst the sheer chaos of the wreckage was arguably the most challenging forensic task of all. Investigators knew they were looking for fragments of electronic circuitry potentially no larger than confetti, possibly damaged or destroyed by the explosion itself. They concentrated their search on debris associated with the Samsonite suitcase and Toshiba radio fragments recovered from the Longtown hangar. Using fine sieves, magnifying glasses, and sometimes even dental picks, they meticulously examined promising pieces of wreckage, particularly those showing signs of proximity to the blast centre. The breakthrough came with the discovery of several tiny, distinct fragments of green fibreglass circuit board material.

One fragment in particular, measuring less than half the size of a postage stamp, attracted intense interest. It was found embedded in a piece of charred material believed to be from the collar of the tweed jacket purchased in Malta, linking it physically to the other key forensic evidence. This crucial fragment, along with others like it, was dispatched under high security for detailed analysis by leading forensic electronics experts, likely including specialists at the UK's RARDE and the FBI's renowned laboratory in Quantico. The examination process was incredibly detailed. Using powerful scanning electron microscopes, analysts mapped the pattern of the copper tracks on the circuit board fragment. They identified the type of solder used and analyzed the composition of the fibreglass substrate. They noted the design style, the thickness of the board, and the remnants of any attached components or solder pads. This micro-detailed information was then compared against extensive reference libraries containing technical specifications for thousands of electronic devices, including known timing mechanisms used in ordnance and improvised explosive devices. The comparison yielded a match. The distinctive track pattern and characteristics of the fragment were unequivocally identified as belonging to an MST-13 digital electronic timer.

The identification of the timer as an MST-13 immediately directed the investigation towards Switzerland and the company MEBO AG (Meister & Bollier AG) in Zurich, the known manufacturer of this device. The MST-13 was not a common, off-the-shelf timer; it was a relatively sophisticated piece of equipment designed for precision and reliability, making it attractive to military or intelligence agencies requiring accurate timing for demolitions or other operations.

Unlike simpler timers, the MST-13 allowed for a countdown interval to be programmed digitally, offering flexibility and precision measured in minutes or even seconds over potentially long durations. Investigators from Scotland and the US, working through Swiss authorities via formal mutual legal assistance channels, descended upon MEBO AG. The company, run by its co-founders Edwin Bollier and Erwin Meister, operated in the often opaque world of supplying specialized electronic and security equipment to international clients, including governments in the Middle East and Africa. Initial interactions with Bollier and Meister were cautious. However, examination of MEBO's business records, combined with statements from the partners and employees, produced the investigation's single most critical piece of evidence linking the bomb directly to a state sponsor.

MEBO confirmed that they had manufactured the MST-13 timers. Crucially, they stated – and company records appeared to corroborate – that a specific batch of these timers, identical in design and manufacturing characteristics to the fragment recovered from the Lockerbie wreckage, had been produced under an exclusive contract for, and delivered solely to, the Libyan government, specifically entities associated with Libyan military intelligence, including the JSO. According to MEBO records and testimony, these timers were part of a larger order for electronic equipment placed by Libya. No other customer, MEBO asserted, had received MST-13 timers of this exact specification. This discovery was the forensic equivalent of finding a fingerprint at a crime scene that matched only one suspect on file. It provided a direct, physical link between the triggering mechanism of the Pan Am 103 bomb and the Gaddafi regime.

The role and testimony of Edwin Bollier and Erwin Meister would become increasingly complex and contentious in the years leading up to and during the eventual trial. Questions would be raised about their business practices, the reliability of their records, and the consistency of their statements. Bollier, in particular, would offer various, sometimes contradictory, accounts regarding the timers, potential modifications, and alleged thefts, providing fodder for defence challenges. However, in the initial phase of the investigation, the core finding presented by MEBO – the exclusive supply of the specific MST-13 timer type to Libya – was treated as a monumental breakthrough by Operation Hornbeam. It appeared to be the 'golden thread' investigators had been searching for.

The convergence of the forensic trails was powerful. The clothing fragments pointed to Malta. The timer fragment pointed to MEBO in Switzerland, who in turn pointed exclusively to Libya. This narrative was further strengthened by the identification of Semtex as the explosive, a material known to be held in significant quantities by Libya and previously supplied by them to terrorist groups like the IRA. The painstaking work conducted in the Longtown hangar and forensic laboratories across the UK and US had transformed the investigation. What began as sifting through wreckage had yielded tangible clues leading across international borders. The focus of Operation Hornbeam now sharpened considerably. While the 'how' (bomb in a suitcase) was becoming clearer, the forensic evidence now provided strong pointers towards the 'who' and the 'where'. The investigation now had a primary suspect state – Libya – and a potential point of origin for the bomb's journey – Malta.

The challenge ahead was to build upon this forensic foundation, to identify the individuals responsible, and to reconstruct the conspiracy behind the destruction of Pan Am 103. The Maltese fragment, in all its forms, had provided the key.

Chapter 6: Zeroing In

The forensic breakthroughs detailed in the previous chapter – the Semtex residues, the Toshiba radio fragments, the clothing traced to Malta, and the definitive link between the MST-13 timer fragment and exclusive Libyan procurement via the Swiss firm MEBO – acted like a powerful lens, bringing the sprawling Lockerbie investigation into sharp focus. While the painstaking recovery work continued across the scarred landscape of southern Scotland, and the meticulous analysis of wreckage proceeded in the Longtown hangar, the central thrust of Operation Hornbeam underwent a crucial transformation. The question was no longer simply what had destroyed Pan Am 103, but who had orchestrated this act of mass murder. The converging lines of physical evidence pointed overwhelmingly towards Muammar Gaddafi's Libya. Now, investigators from Dumfries and Galloway Constabulary and the FBI faced the immense challenge of penetrating the opaque structures of the Libyan state, particularly its intelligence apparatus, to identify the specific individuals responsible. This required navigating the complex, often ambiguous world of international intelligence, cross-referencing covert information with travel records, financial transactions, and witness statements, gradually zeroing in on the names that would become synonymous with the Lockerbie bombing.

Intelligence Whispers: Sources and Suspicions

The intense focus on Libya following the forensic discoveries did not occur in an intelligence vacuum. Western intelligence agencies had been monitoring Gaddafi's regime for years, building up a detailed, if incomplete, picture of its capabilities, intentions, and methods. They were well aware of Libya's deep-seated animosity towards the US and UK, fueled by incidents like the 1986 Operation El Dorado Canyon airstrikes. They knew Libya possessed significant stockpiles of Semtex plastic explosive, acquired from Czechoslovakia. They understood the structure of Libyan intelligence, primarily the Jamahiriya Security Organization (JSO) and its external operations wing (later ESO), known to be involved in assassinating dissidents abroad (the "stray dog" campaign) and providing extensive support – training, funding, weapons, logistics – to a wide array of international terrorist groups, including radical Palestinian factions and the IRA. Key figures within the Libyan intelligence hierarchy, such as Abdullah Senussi (Gaddafi's brother-in-law and a feared intelligence chief), were known quantities, albeit often operating from the shadows.

The immediate aftermath of Lockerbie triggered an unprecedented surge in intelligence gathering directed at Libya. Signals intelligence (SIGINT) platforms operated by agencies like the US National Security Agency (NSA) and Britain's Government Communications Headquarters (GCHQ) intensified monitoring of Libyan diplomatic, military, and intelligence communications, searching for any hint of involvement, celebratory chatter, or attempts at concealment.

Human intelligence (HUMINT) assets – agents recruited within or close to the Libyan regime – were tasked with reporting any relevant information regarding the government's reaction, internal discussions about the bombing, or unusual activities within the JSO/ESO. Covert surveillance of known Libyan operatives in Europe and elsewhere was likely increased. Allied intelligence agencies pooled their resources and findings, sharing reports and assessments through established liaison channels, although such sharing is often carefully managed due to concerns about source protection and differing national priorities. The challenge for intelligence analysts was immense: to sift through potentially vast amounts of raw data – intercepted messages often using code or oblique language, reports from human sources of varying reliability, satellite imagery, diplomatic reports – looking for patterns, connections, and credible leads that could corroborate the emerging forensic evidence and point towards specific perpetrators.

While the forensic evidence increasingly pointed towards Libya, the intelligence picture in the initial weeks and months remained complex, forcing investigators to keep other possibilities in consideration. The theory involving Iranian revenge for the downing of Iran Air 655, possibly executed by the PFLP-GC with Syrian support, could not be immediately dismissed. This theory gained some traction due to several factors: Iran certainly had a powerful motive; the PFLP-GC, led by Ahmed Jibril and based in Damascus, had proven expertise in building sophisticated bombs concealed in electronic devices (specifically, Toshiba radio cassette players similar to the Lockerbie device); and German authorities had arrested members of a PFLP-GC cell in October 1988 (just two months before Lockerbie) in an operation codenamed 'Autumn Leaves', seizing several such bombs already constructed. Intelligence reports suggested this cell might have been targeting Iberia Airlines flights serving US military personnel. Could the Lockerbie bomb have been a PFLP-GC device that slipped through the net, perhaps rerouted towards Pan Am after the German arrests disrupted their initial plans? Was there an Iranian financial link? Did Syria facilitate the operation? These questions were actively pursued by intelligence agencies and investigators. Liaison with German authorities (the BKA) regarding the Autumn Leaves investigation was crucial. However, several factors eventually led the mainstream investigation, particularly the joint UK-US Operation Hornbeam team, to discount this theory in favour of the Libyan connection. Key PFLP-GC figures were reportedly under surveillance and did not appear to be activating operations around the time of Lockerbie; the specific type of timer fragment (MST-13) found in the Lockerbie wreckage did not match the timers associated with the PFLP-GC devices seized in Germany (which typically used barometric or simpler electronic timers); and most importantly, the forensic trail leading to Malta and the exclusive Libyan procurement of the MST-13 timers provided a more direct, tangible link than the circumstantial evidence supporting the PFLP-GC/Iran hypothesis.

While proponents of the alternative theory remained vocal, arguing that the focus on Libya might have been politically convenient, the official investigation increasingly concentrated its resources based on the weight of the physical evidence pointing towards Tripoli. Intelligence analysis also focused heavily on the known modus operandi of Libyan intelligence. The JSO/ESO frequently used Libyan Arab Airlines (LAA) as both cover and a logistical tool.

Operatives often held official positions within the airline, allowing them legitimate access to airports, aircraft, and international travel. LAA offices abroad sometimes doubled as intelligence outposts. False passports and aliases were common tools of the trade. Operations were often compartmentalized, with different cells or individuals handling specific tasks (e.g., surveillance, procurement, bomb-making, delivery) without necessarily knowing the full picture, enhancing operational security and deniability. Understanding these methods helped investigators interpret travel patterns, identify potential operatives travelling under LAA cover, and anticipate how a bomb might have been moved through the airline system. Intelligence reports detailing previous Libyan operations involving explosives, timers, or targeting aviation provided valuable context. As the investigation progressed, specific intelligence reports, perhaps from defectors or technical intercepts (though details remain classified), likely began to surface, potentially mentioning internal discussions within the JSO/ESO about an operation against a US target, or highlighting the movements of specific operatives in key locations like Malta or Switzerland during the relevant timeframe. While such intelligence might not constitute stand-alone proof for a court, it provided crucial direction for the police and FBI investigators, helping them to prioritize leads and focus on individuals whose profiles and activities matched the emerging picture.

Naming Names: The Emergence of Megrahi and Fhimah

With the forensic evidence pointing strongly to a Libyan-orchestrated plot originating in Malta, and intelligence providing context about Libyan methods and potential involvement, Operation Hornbeam investigators began the critical task of identifying the specific individuals who bridged these elements. They needed to find Libyan operatives who had access to the MST-13 timer, who were present in Malta during the period the bomb was likely prepared and planted, who had the means and opportunity to introduce an unaccompanied suitcase into the baggage system at Luqa Airport, and whose travel patterns might connect these different locations and activities. This involved painstakingly correlating intelligence data with forensic timelines, airline passenger records, immigration logs, hotel registrations, and witness statements gathered across multiple countries.

The name Abdelbaset Ali Mohmed al-Megrahi emerged as a figure of significant interest early on. Born in Tripoli in 1952 and belonging to the influential Magarha tribe (a factor of some significance within Libya's complex social structure), Megrahi was well-educated, reportedly having studied in the United States and the UK in the 1970s. Officially, he held senior positions within Libyan Arab Airlines, serving for a time as the airline's chief of security – a role that would have given him intimate knowledge of international aviation security protocols and vulnerabilities. At the time of the bombing, he was listed as the Director of the Centre for Strategic Studies in Tripoli, a title potentially serving as cover for his more clandestine activities.

Western intelligence agencies had long suspected Megrahi was not just an airline executive but a senior officer within the JSO/ESO, involved in intelligence gathering and covert procurement operations overseas. His LAA role provided the perfect justification for frequent travel throughout Europe, the Middle East, and Africa. Investigators began meticulously reconstructing his movements in the months leading up to December 1988. They uncovered records showing numerous trips, sometimes under his own name, sometimes allegedly using aliases such as 'Ahmed Khalifa Abdusamad'. Of particular interest were trips that placed him in Switzerland, potentially liaising with MEBO AG regarding the MST-13 timers (investigators explored evidence suggesting Megrahi had prior dealings with Edwin Bollier), and crucially, trips placing him in Malta during late November and early December 1988, coinciding with the timeframe Tony Gauci recalled selling the clothing later found in the bomb suitcase.

The second key name to surface was Lamin Khalifah Fhimah. Born in 1956, Fhimah served as the station manager for Libyan Arab Airlines at Luqa Airport in Malta throughout 1988. Unlike Megrahi, Fhimah was not initially believed to be a high-ranking intelligence officer, but his position was strategically vital. As the LAA station manager, he possessed an airside security pass granting him unrestricted access to all areas of Luqa Airport, including baggage handling facilities, customs areas, and the tarmac itself. He would have had detailed knowledge of flight schedules, cargo manifests, security routines, and baggage transfer procedures for both LAA and other airlines operating out of Malta, including Air Malta.

If the bomb suitcase needed to be introduced into the baggage system at Luqa, specifically onto Air Malta flight KM180 to Frankfurt, without being screened or reconciled with a boarding passenger, Fhimah's access and authority could have been instrumental, perhaps essential, in facilitating this crucial step. Investigators focused intensely on Fhimah's activities at the airport, interviewing his colleagues, subordinates, and staff from other airlines and airport services. They examined LAA records from the Malta station and looked for any evidence linking Fhimah directly to Megrahi or other suspected JSO/ESO operatives active on the island. Intelligence suggesting Fhimah might have JSO connections, or witness accounts placing him in contact with Megrahi during his visits to Malta, became critical lines of inquiry.

The identification of Megrahi by Tony Gauci provided a seemingly direct link between one of the emerging suspects and the physical preparation of the bomb. The process, however, was complex and became highly contentious. After Gauci's initial interviews where he described the clothing purchaser, investigators compiled photographic arrays containing pictures of potential suspects, including Megrahi, alongside individuals with similar appearances (fillers). Over several sessions, Gauci was asked if he could identify the man. His responses were initially hesitant. Critically, before making a positive identification during a formal session in September 1989, Gauci saw a photograph of Megrahi published in a magazine article explicitly linking him to the Lockerbie investigation. Defence lawyers would later argue vehemently that this exposure fatally tainted the identification, rendering it unreliable due to suggestion.

However, at the time, the investigators recorded Gauci's eventual positive identification of Megrahi from the photo array as a major breakthrough, apparently corroborating Megrahi's presence in Malta and his direct involvement in acquiring items packed into the bomb suitcase. This eyewitness evidence, however flawed it might later appear under legal scrutiny, became a central pillar supporting the indictment against Megrahi.

Alongside the Gauci identification, investigators devoted enormous resources to tracking the precise movements of both Megrahi and Fhimah. This involved obtaining and analyzing a vast array of records from multiple countries: airline ticket stubs, passenger name records (PNRs) which contain detailed booking information, passport stamps showing border crossings, visa applications, hotel registration cards (often requiring meticulous handwriting analysis), car rental receipts, telephone records, and financial transaction data. They focused intently on the period from late November 1988, when the clothing was likely purchased, through December 21st. They identified specific flights Megrahi allegedly took, including travel under the 'Abdusamad' alias that placed him in Zurich around the time investigators believed the timer might have been procured or finalized, and crucially, flights placing him in Malta on dates consistent with the clothing purchase and potential meetings with Fhimah. Similarly, Fhimah's work records confirmed his presence and duties at Luqa Airport throughout this period.

While investigators couldn't construct an unbroken chain showing every moment of their alleged conspiracy, they assembled a compelling circumstantial case based on placing both men in the right locations at the right times, possessing the necessary means and access, consistent with the prosecution's developing theory of their respective roles.

Based on this complex mosaic of converging evidence – the definitive forensic links to Libya via the timer and Semtex; the forensic link to Malta via the clothing; the contested eyewitness identification of Megrahi in Malta; intelligence assessments of Libyan capabilities, motives, and the suspects' alleged JSO/LAA roles; and the painstakingly reconstructed travel records – the joint Scottish-US investigation team concluded they had identified the two individuals directly responsible for planting the bomb. The narrative they constructed, which would form the basis for indictment, was that Megrahi, the senior intelligence operative, planned the operation, obtained the timer, travelled to Malta to oversee the bomb's preparation (including purchasing the clothing for concealment), and potentially assembled or supervised the assembly of the device. Fhimah, the LAA station manager with crucial airport access, then allegedly used his position at Luqa Airport to ensure the unaccompanied suitcase containing the bomb bypassed security checks and was loaded onto the Air Malta flight to Frankfurt on the morning of December 21st, setting in motion the chain of events that led to the destruction of Pan Am 103 hours later. By late 1990 and early 1991, after extensive internal reviews within the Crown Office in Scotland and the US Department of Justice, prosecutors determined that sufficient evidence existed to bring formal charges.

The long, complex investigation, born amidst the horror of Lockerbie, had zeroed in on its targets. The next challenge would be to secure their presence for trial and test this evidence in court.

Chapter 7: Standoff

The announcement on November 14, 1991, represented far more than just a significant development in a complex criminal investigation; it was a moment of profound international consequence. After almost three years of meticulous, often frustrating, work by thousands of investigators, scientists, police officers, and intelligence analysts operating under the banner of Operation Hornbeam, formal accusations were levelled against two Libyan nationals for the bombing of Pan Am Flight 103. The simultaneous declarations in Edinburgh and Washington D.C., naming Abdelbaset Ali Mohmed al-Megrahi and Lamin Khalifah Fhimah as agents of the Libyan state responsible for murdering 270 people, drew a clear line in the sand. It transformed the Lockerbie tragedy from a devastating, unsolved mystery into a direct confrontation between major Western powers and Muammar Gaddafi's Libya. The demand for the suspects' extradition to face trial in Scotland or the United States was unequivocal. Yet, Libya's immediate and defiant refusal plunged the situation into a protracted standoff, a decade-long test of international resolve, diplomatic maneuvering, economic pressure, and the enduring power of bereaved families demanding justice against formidable political obstacles.

Indictment Issued: Justice Demanded, Justice Denied

The decision to proceed with indictments was not taken lightly. Within Scotland's Crown Office, Lord Advocate Allan Stewart and his team of senior prosecutors, including Advocates Depute who would eventually argue the case in court, subjected the vast dossier of evidence compiled by Dumfries and Galloway Constabulary and its partners to rigorous scrutiny. Under Scottish law, the test was stringent: was there sufficient credible and admissible evidence to establish a prima facie case against the accused, strong enough to justify committal for trial with realistic prospects of conviction? This involved assessing the forensic evidence (the timer fragment, the clothing link to Malta, the Semtex traces), the controversial eyewitness identification provided by Tony Gauci, the complex web of travel records and aliases, and potentially sensitive intelligence assessments regarding the suspects' roles within Libyan intelligence (JSO/ESO) and their connections to the Libyan state.

Concurrently, across the Atlantic, the US Department of Justice, under the oversight of Assistant Attorney General Robert Mueller and ultimately Attorney General William Barr, conducted its own exhaustive review. They assessed the evidence against the standards required for a US federal indictment (probable cause) and framed charges under specific US statutes dealing with terrorism, aviation sabotage, and the murder of American citizens overseas. The unprecedented level of cooperation during the investigation phase continued into this pre-indictment legal review, ensuring both jurisdictions were confident in the evidence and aligned in their approach, anticipating the inevitable international legal and diplomatic battles ahead.

The joint conclusion was clear: the evidence, though heavily circumstantial in parts, particularly regarding Fhimah, met the necessary thresholds to formally charge both men. The public unveiling on November 14th was carefully choreographed. In Edinburgh, Lord Advocate Stewart addressed the media, formally confirming the issue of petitions seeking warrants for the arrest of Megrahi and Fhimah on charges of conspiracy and 270 counts of murder. He summarized the core elements of the investigation's findings, highlighting the forensic trail leading to Malta and the timer link to Libya, emphasizing the belief that the two accused acted "in furtherance of the objectives of the Libyan Intelligence Services." In Washington, Assistant Attorney General Mueller delivered a parallel statement, detailing the US federal indictment and emphasizing the American commitment to pursuing justice for its murdered citizens. Mueller stated bluntly, "The investigation reveals that the bombing of Pan Am 103 was not a random act of violence... It was the calculated result of a conspiracy directed by officials of the Libyan government."

The specific charges detailed in the US indictment included Conspiracy to Destroy an Aircraft; Destruction of an Aircraft Resulting in Death; Causing the Bombing Deaths of 270 People; Conspiracy to Murder US Nationals; Murder of US Nationals; and Placing a Destructive Device on an Aircraft. Both announcements underscored the belief that this was an act of state-sponsored terrorism, directly implicating the Gaddafi regime. Formal requests for the extradition of both men were immediately transmitted to the Libyan government through diplomatic channels.

Libya's response was one of outright rejection and furious denunciation. The Libyan Foreign Ministry (the People's Bureau for Foreign Liaison and International Cooperation) issued statements dismissing the charges as politically motivated slander, lacking any credible evidence and representing a continuation of American and British aggression against Libya. Muammar Gaddafi himself, in speeches and interviews broadcast by Libyan state media, portrayed his country as the victim of an international conspiracy, falsely accused by arrogant imperialist powers. He denied any Libyan involvement whatsoever in the Lockerbie bombing. Libya refused point-blank to consider extraditing Megrahi and Fhimah, citing national sovereignty and asserting that Libyan citizens accused of crimes should be tried, if anywhere, within Libya's own judicial system according to Libyan law.

They invoked the 1971 Montreal Convention for the Suppression of Unlawful Acts against the Safety of Civil Aviation, arguing that under its terms, Libya had the right to prosecute the suspects domestically rather than extradite them. Libyan authorities announced they were launching their own investigation and declared that Megrahi and Fhimah had been placed under judicial supervision or 'house arrest' pending its outcome. However, this was widely perceived internationally as a cosmetic measure designed to shield the suspects, who were occasionally seen moving relatively freely within Libya, seemingly under the protection of the regime. Libya also mounted a significant propaganda campaign, particularly within the Arab world and Africa, portraying the US/UK demands as an attack on Arab solidarity and Third World independence.

The international community's reaction was largely predictable. The US and UK governments, under President George H.W. Bush and Prime Minister John Major respectively, issued strong statements reiterating their demands for extradition and warning of consequences should Libya fail to comply. They received firm backing from key Western allies like France (already pursuing Libya over the UTA 772 bombing), Germany, Canada, and Australia. These nations accepted the findings of the joint investigation and supported the call for the suspects to face trial in either Scotland or the US. However, the response from other parts of the world was more varied. The Arab League expressed concern but stopped short of condemning Libya outright, calling for a solution that respected Libyan sovereignty. Some African nations, influenced by Gaddafi's long-standing projection of himself as an anti-colonial leader and provider of aid, offered diplomatic support or mediation proposals that fell short of demanding extradition. Russia, navigating the chaotic collapse of the Soviet Union, played a relatively minor role initially. China generally advocated for resolving the issue through dialogue rather than confrontation. This mixed international reaction highlighted the difficulty of achieving universal consensus against a state accused of terrorism when geopolitical interests and historical alignments came into play.

For the families of the victims, the indictments represented a watershed moment, albeit one fraught with complex emotions. There was immense relief that after nearly three years of campaigning, demanding answers, and grappling with their loss, specific individuals had finally been named and formally accused. It validated their belief that the bombing was a deliberate act, not a tragic accident, and offered a concrete focus for their pursuit of justice.

Spokespersons for UK Families Flight 103 and the US-based Victims of Pan Am Flight 103 publicly welcomed the indictments but immediately pivoted to expressing outrage at Libya's refusal to extradite. They recognized that naming the suspects was only the beginning. The real challenge lay in bringing them before a court. The family groups, already highly organized and effective lobbying forces, intensified their activities. They held press conferences, met with senior officials at the US State Department, the British Foreign Office, and the UN, demanding that their governments maintain unwavering pressure on Libya and reject any compromises that did not involve a credible criminal trial. They shared their stories, put human faces to the abstract geopolitical conflict, and served as a constant moral compass, ensuring that the pursuit of justice for the 270 victims remained a high priority for policymakers in Washington and London. Their determination was absolute: justice demanded a trial, and Libya's defiance would not be allowed to stand unchallenged.

Years of Sanctions: Libya Under Pressure

With Libya resolutely refusing extradition and initial diplomatic pressure yielding no results, the United States and the United Kingdom shifted their strategy towards coercive measures through the United Nations. The goal was to impose significant costs on the Gaddafi regime for its non-compliance, hoping to compel it to hand over Megrahi and Fhimah. This involved leveraging their influence as permanent members of the UN Security Council to frame Libya's actions as a threat to international peace and security, thereby justifying mandatory sanctions under Chapter VII of the UN Charter – a powerful tool reserved for situations deemed to endanger global stability. Intense diplomatic activity took place in late 1991 and early 1992, with US, UK, and French diplomats working to build consensus within the Security Council. They presented detailed briefings on the Lockerbie investigation findings and the parallel French investigation into the UTA 772 bombing, arguing that Libya's pattern of state-sponsored terrorism required a robust international response.

The first step came in January 1992 with the unanimous adoption of UN Security Council Resolution 731. This resolution formally noted the charges against the two Libyan nationals, expressed deep concern over Libya's failure to cooperate fully in establishing responsibility for the Lockerbie bombing (and the UTA bombing), and urged the Libyan government "to provide a full and effective response" to the requests for extradition and cooperation "without delay." It was a clear international condemnation and demand, but crucially, it did not yet invoke Chapter VII or impose mandatory sanctions.

It represented a final diplomatic warning. Libya's response was unchanged: continued denials, offers of alternative trial venues deemed unacceptable by the US/UK, and accusations of political bias. This predictable defiance paved the way for stronger action. On March 31, 1992, the Security Council adopted Resolution 748, explicitly acting under Chapter VII. This resolution determined that Libya's continued failure to comply with Resolution 731 constituted a threat to international peace and security. It mandated a series of tough sanctions, binding on all UN member states, to take effect on April 15, 1992. These included: a comprehensive air embargo, prohibiting all flights into or out of Libya and barring Libyan Arab Airlines from operating internationally; a stringent arms embargo, banning the sale or supply of weapons, military equipment, and related technical assistance to Libya; and a requirement for all states to significantly reduce the level and number of staff at Libyan diplomatic missions in their territories and restrict the activities of remaining personnel.

The aim was clear: to isolate Libya physically, politically, and militarily, making it increasingly difficult for the regime to conduct normal international relations or pursue its foreign policy objectives. The flight ban, in particular, had an immediate impact, forcing Libyans seeking to travel abroad to undertake arduous overland journeys to neighbouring countries like Tunisia or Egypt to access international airports. Despite the unprecedented pressure of mandatory UN sanctions, Gaddafi refused to budge on the core issue of extradition. While Libya made occasional gestures – allowing Scottish investigators limited access to interview witnesses in Tripoli, continuing to float alternative trial proposals – it never wavered in its refusal to hand over Megrahi and Fhimah to face trial in Scotland or the US.

The regime appeared willing to endure the economic and political isolation, possibly believing it could ride out the storm, perhaps calculating that divisions within the international community would eventually weaken the sanctions regime, or simply prioritizing the protection of its own operatives (and potentially shielding higher-level state involvement) above all else. As Libya's non-compliance persisted, the Security Council decided to increase the pressure further. In November 1993, Resolution 883 was adopted, again under Chapter VII. This resolution significantly tightened the existing sanctions: it ordered the freezing of Libyan government financial funds and assets held abroad (though carefully exempting revenues derived directly from oil, gas, and agricultural sales to avoid triggering a full-blown humanitarian crisis or destabilizing global oil markets); it prohibited the sale or supply to Libya of specific categories of large-scale equipment essential for oil transportation, refining, and export terminals (such as large-diameter pipes, pumps, and certain types of drilling equipment), aiming to degrade Libya's capacity to profit from its main export over the long term; and it reinforced the air embargo by requiring the closure of all LAA offices worldwide and banning the provision of aircraft engineering and maintenance services to Libyan aircraft.

The cumulative impact of these sanctions, maintained and enforced throughout the mid-to-late 1990s, undeniably inflicted hardship on Libya. The economy suffered from the restrictions on importing equipment and technology, particularly impacting the vital oil sector's development and maintenance. Major infrastructure projects languished. Ordinary Libyans faced significant difficulties with international travel, access to imported goods, and sometimes specialized medical care that required travel abroad. Inflation and unemployment reportedly rose. The country's international isolation deepened. However, the regime proved remarkably resilient. Gaddafi used the sanctions to rally nationalist sentiment, blaming Libya's woes entirely on external enemies. The continued flow of oil revenue, even with restrictions on equipment, provided the state with sufficient funds to maintain its security apparatus, provide basic subsidies, and prevent widespread popular unrest. Gaddafi skillfully played diplomatic games, making occasional conciliatory noises or offering compensation deals through intermediaries (always careful to avoid admitting legal responsibility) to test international resolve or exploit potential divisions among Security Council members. Libya challenged the legality of the sanctions at the International Court of Justice, arguing they violated the Montreal Convention, though the court ultimately ruled the Security Council resolutions took precedence. For years, the situation remained locked in a frustrating stalemate.

Throughout this prolonged period, the victims' families remained a constant, powerful voice demanding justice. They became adept political operators, maintaining relentless pressure on their own governments through lobbying, letter-writing campaigns, media appearances, and annual memorial services that served as poignant reminders of the unresolved crime. They countered Libyan propaganda, challenged arguments for easing sanctions prematurely, and insisted that any resolution must include a criminal trial before a credible court. Groups like UK Families Flight 103 and Victims of Pan Am Flight 103 worked tirelessly to ensure that successive administrations in Washington (under President Bill Clinton) and London (under Prime Ministers John Major and later Tony Blair) did not allow the Lockerbie issue to slip down the foreign policy agenda. They met frequently with diplomats, members of Congress and Parliament, and UN officials, articulating the human cost of the bombing and the moral imperative of accountability. Their persistence, dignity, and refusal to be silenced played an indispensable role in maintaining international pressure on Libya and keeping alive the possibility, however distant it often seemed during the long years of standoff, that Megrahi and Fhimah would one day face their accusers in court. The indictments had initiated the confrontation, the sanctions had defined its terms, but the unwavering resolve of the families ensured the pursuit of justice endured through the deadlock.

Chapter 8: The Deal for Trial

The years dragged on. From 1991 into the latter half of the 1990s, the Lockerbie bombing case remained frozen in a state of intractable diplomatic confrontation. The indictments against Abdelbaset al-Megrahi and Lamin Khalifah Fhimah stood, yet the accused remained safely ensconced in Libya, shielded from extradition by the defiant regime of Muammar Gaddafi. The United Nations sanctions, progressively tightened under Resolutions 731, 748, and 883, inflicted demonstrable economic pain and international isolation upon Libya, yet they failed to achieve their primary objective: compelling Gaddafi to surrender the suspects for trial in Scotland or the United States. Washington and London, under consistent, unrelenting pressure from the vocal and well-organized victims' families, refused to countenance any compromise that fell short of a credible judicial process under their respective legal systems. Libya, in turn, portrayed itself as a victim of Western persecution, refusing to yield its citizens to what it claimed would be a politically motivated show trial. Diplomatic initiatives flickered and died. Proposals and counter-proposals were exchanged through intermediaries, only to founder on the bedrock issues of sovereignty, jurisdiction, and mutual distrust. The situation seemed locked in perpetual stalemate, a testament to the difficulty of achieving international justice when faced with the resistance of a determined state actor, even one isolated by global consensus. Yet, beneath the surface of this apparent impasse, complex forces were subtly shifting, creating openings for new diplomatic approaches that would eventually, painstakingly, lead to an unexpected and unprecedented resolution.

Diplomatic Breakthroughs: Mandela, Annan, and the Path to Trial

The persistence of the stalemate stemmed from deeply entrenched positions. For Gaddafi, handing over two alleged Libyan intelligence officers, particularly figures like Megrahi with potentially extensive knowledge of the regime's operations, represented an enormous political risk. It could be perceived domestically as capitulation to Western pressure, undermining his revolutionary credentials. More crucially, it risked opening a Pandora's Box, potentially revealing direct state complicity at higher levels in the Lockerbie bombing and perhaps other terrorist acts, leading to further international condemnation and possibly demands for Gaddafi himself to face justice.

His refusal to extradite was likely rooted in self-preservation as much as national pride or concern for the suspects' fate. Conversely, for the US and UK governments, any compromise that appeared to offer impunity for state-sponsored terrorism was politically untenable, particularly given the scale of the atrocity and the ceaseless campaigning by the victims' families who demanded nothing less than a full criminal trial. Furthermore, maintaining the credibility of international law and UN Security Council resolutions required demonstrating that defiance carried a significant, sustained cost. The sanctions, therefore, became both a tool of coercion and a symbol of international resolve, difficult to lift without tangible progress on the extradition issue. Some observers also noted a potential 'sanctions fatigue' setting in within parts of the international community by the mid-to-late 1990s, with growing debate about their humanitarian impact on ordinary Libyans and their effectiveness in changing the regime's behaviour, adding pressure to find a diplomatic off-ramp. Against this complex backdrop, subtle shifts began to occur within Libya itself. The cumulative effect of years of sanctions, particularly the restrictions on oil industry equipment imposed by Resolution 883, started to bite more deeply, hindering Libya's ability to maintain, let alone expand, its primary source of national wealth. Gaddafi, ever the pragmatist beneath the revolutionary rhetoric, likely recognised the long-term unsustainability of Libya's isolation. His ambitions to play a leading role in African and Arab affairs were hampered, and the desire for international rehabilitation, including attracting foreign investment and technology, grew stronger. Furthermore, internal dynamics within Libya, including potential concerns about succession planning or managing dissent, might have contributed to a reassessment of the costs versus benefits of continuing the Lockerbie standoff indefinitely. Libyan diplomats began discreetly signalling a greater willingness to explore creative solutions, provided Libya's core concerns about sovereignty and ensuring a fair trial for its citizens could be addressed.

The crucial breakthroughs, however, came through the dedicated intervention of high-profile, trusted intermediaries operating outside the direct US-UK-Libya axis. Nelson Mandela's role was pivotal. Emerging from 27 years of imprisonment to lead South Africa's transition to democracy, Mandela commanded unparalleled global respect. His relationship with Gaddafi was complex; Libya had been a vocal supporter and financial backer of the ANC during the struggle against apartheid, and Mandela felt a degree of loyalty and gratitude.

This unique position allowed him access and influence in Tripoli that Western leaders lacked. Starting in 1997, Mandela made several high-profile visits to Libya, engaging in lengthy, face-to-face negotiations with Gaddafi. Leveraging his immense moral authority, Mandela argued passionately that resolving the Lockerbie issue was not only essential for lifting the sanctions that were harming the Libyan people but also crucial for upholding principles of international justice. He reportedly spent hours patiently listening to Gaddafi's grievances and fears about a biased trial, while firmly insisting that the suspects must face due process. Mandela acted as a crucial bridge, relaying messages, exploring compromises, and using his global stature to reassure both Libya and the West.

His involvement lent significant weight and credibility to the search for a negotiated solution. Simultaneously, Saudi Arabia played a vital, though less public, role. Prince Bandar bin Sultan, the long-serving and highly influential Saudi ambassador in Washington, utilized his extensive contacts within the US administration, the UK government, and the Libyan regime to act as a key facilitator. Saudi diplomacy helped to broker secret meetings, test proposals, and build the necessary confidence between the parties, leveraging Saudi Arabia's position as a major Arab power respected by both sides.

Through these intensive, often clandestine, diplomatic efforts, the concept of a "third way" trial began to crystallize. The core idea, potentially floated in various forms earlier but now gaining serious traction, was trial in a neutral third country. This directly addressed Libya's primary objection to trial in the US or Scotland, offering a venue perceived as less politically charged and potentially more impartial.

However, to satisfy the absolute insistence of the US and UK on legal credibility, the trial had to operate under either Scottish or US law. Given that the crime culminated over Scotland and the bulk of the evidence had been gathered under Scottish jurisdiction, the proposal solidified around a trial conducted fully under Scottish law, adhering to Scottish rules of evidence and procedure, and presided over by Scottish High Court judges. The idea of dispensing with a jury, highly unusual for a Scottish murder trial but permissible under specific circumstances with parliamentary approval, was introduced as a further concession to Libyan concerns about potential juror bias in such a high-profile, emotionally charged case. The Netherlands emerged as the preferred host nation due to its central location, strong tradition of international law (hosting the International Court of Justice in The Hague), excellent infrastructure, and political willingness to facilitate this unique arrangement. The Dutch government signalled its openness, provided appropriate legal and security frameworks could be established.

The final, crucial phase of negotiations fell largely to the then UN Secretary-General, Kofi Annan. Building upon the groundwork laid by Mandela and others, Annan engaged in direct, intensive diplomacy throughout 1998 and early 1999. He travelled to Tripoli multiple times, holding critical meetings with Gaddafi and senior Libyan officials. Annan's task was to hammer out the precise details and secure irrevocable commitments from all sides. He had to address Libya's lingering concerns: guarantees regarding the suspects' treatment in detention, the conditions of the trial itself (including access for Libyan observers), arrangements for imprisonment if convicted (agreement was reached on imprisonment in Scotland under UN supervision), and absolute clarity on the linkage between handing over the suspects and the suspension of UN sanctions. Simultaneously, Annan had to ensure the arrangements fully satisfied the non-negotiable demands of the US and UK for a trial conducted under Scottish law with full judicial independence and integrity. His role required immense diplomatic skill – building personal rapport, navigating cultural sensitivities, patiently exploring wording for agreements, and leveraging the moral and political authority of the United Nations. Annan also maintained close communication with the victims' family groups, explaining the proposed compromise, listening to their concerns, and seeking their acceptance, which was politically vital for the US and UK governments. While divisions remained among the families – some accepting the deal as the best achievable path to justice, others remaining deeply opposed to any deviation from trial in Scotland or the US – Annan's efforts helped secure enough understanding to allow the process to move forward. Finally, after months of intense back-and-forth, a comprehensive agreement was reached, formally documented in exchanges of letters between the UN, Libya, the US, the UK, and the Netherlands. Libya committed to transferring the suspects to the Netherlands by a specified date; the US and UK committed to the trial proceeding under the agreed conditions and to the immediate suspension of UN sanctions upon the suspects' arrival. The diplomatic logjam was broken.

A Scottish Court on Dutch Soil: Preparing the Unprecedented

The diplomatic agreement, while a monumental achievement, set in motion an equally challenging phase: the practical implementation of establishing a fully functioning Scottish High Court on Dutch territory. This required unprecedented legal innovation and a massive logistical undertaking, executed under intense time pressure and global scrutiny. The first hurdle was establishing the legal framework. Holding a Scottish criminal trial outside Scotland required specific primary legislation passed by the UK Parliament in London (as significant criminal justice matters were still largely reserved from the nascent Scottish Parliament). The resulting High Court of Justiciary (Proceedings in the Netherlands) (United Nations) Order 1998 formally empowered the Scottish High Court to sit in the Netherlands, granted the judges their full powers and immunities, and made provisions for applying Scottish law and procedure extraterritorially. Complementary legislation was swiftly passed by the Dutch Parliament, formally designating the agreed site – a section of the former US airbase at Camp Zeist, near Utrecht – as sovereign territory under the jurisdiction of the Scottish court for the duration of the proceedings. This clever legal device created an enclave where Scottish law reigned supreme, overcoming the complex sovereignty issues inherent in conducting one nation's criminal trial within another's borders.

Camp Zeist itself required a radical transformation. Chosen for its secure perimeter and existing infrastructure, the site nonetheless needed extensive adaptation. A budget running into tens of millions of pounds, primarily funded by the US and UK, was allocated for construction and refurbishment.

The centrepiece was the construction of a brand new, purpose-built courthouse within the secure zone. Architects and engineers worked rapidly to design and erect a building that met the specific requirements of a Scottish High Court trial. This included a courtroom with the correct layout – the elevated bench for the three judges, the witness box positioned for clear audibility and visibility, the secure glass-panelled dock for the two accused, separate areas for the large prosecution and defence legal teams, and galleries capable of accommodating hundreds of observers, including victims' families, accredited media representatives, and diplomatic personnel. Cutting-edge technology was installed, including systems for simultaneous interpretation between English and Arabic, digital audio recording and transcription, secure evidence presentation facilities, and robust external communication links. Adjacent buildings within the Camp Zeist complex were rapidly converted into secure office suites for the judges, prosecution, defence, court administration, police liaison teams, and UN monitors. Secure accommodation blocks were prepared to house Megrahi and Fhimah during the potentially year-long trial, along with facilities for remand prisoners. The entire complex had to be self-contained and capable of operating independently, effectively creating a small, secure judicial village dedicated solely to the Lockerbie trial.

Security considerations permeated every aspect of the planning and construction. The trial of alleged state-sponsored terrorists involved inherent risks, demanding the highest levels of protection. The Dutch government, through its military police (Royal Marechaussee) and national police forces, assumed responsibility for the external security of Camp Zeist, establishing multiple checkpoints, perimeter patrols, and surveillance systems.

Internal security within the designated Scottish territory was managed by a large contingent of specially assigned Scottish police officers, working in coordination with Dutch colleagues and UN security advisors. Every individual entering the complex, regardless of status, underwent stringent security screening. Detailed protocols governed the secure movement of the accused between their accommodation and the courtroom. Measures were put in place to protect the three presiding judges, both within the complex and during their off-duty hours. Contingency plans were developed for various emergency scenarios, from medical incidents to external threats. The sheer logistics of managing secure access for hundreds of participants and observers daily, while maintaining the integrity of the judicial process, required meticulous planning and constant vigilance.

As the physical infrastructure took shape, the human elements of the court were assembled. Three highly experienced Scottish judges were appointed to preside: Lord Sutherland (who initially presided but later stood down due to ill health, being replaced by Lord Cullen as presiding judge), Lord Coulsfield, and Lord MacLean. Their task, sitting without a jury, would be to hear the evidence, determine the facts, and apply complex Scottish law to reach a verdict – a responsibility of immense weight. The Crown Office finalized its prosecution team, led by the Lord Advocate Colin Boyd QC, supported by several senior Advocates Depute and solicitors, tasked with presenting the voluminous and complex case meticulously compiled by Operation Hornbeam. Megrahi and Fhimah, meanwhile, assembled formidable defence teams.

Megrahi was represented by William Taylor QC, one of Scotland's leading defence advocates, assisted by solicitor Alistair Duff and American lawyer Ramsey Clark (a former US Attorney General). Fhimah was represented by Richard Keen QC (later Lord Keen), another top Scottish advocate, backed by solicitors and consultants. The presence of such high-calibre legal teams on both sides ensured the trial would be rigorously contested. An extensive support staff of court clerks (macerators), translators fluent in Arabic and English legal terminology, shorthand writers producing verbatim transcripts, IT specialists, and security personnel were recruited and deployed to Camp Zeist. An independent observer, appointed by the UN Secretary-General, was also present throughout the proceedings to monitor compliance with international standards of fairness.

Finally, after months of intense preparation, the moment arrived. On April 5, 1999, the complex diplomatic agreement reached its tangible conclusion. Abdelbaset al-Megrahi and Lamin Khalifah Fhimah, having been under Libyan 'supervision' for over seven years, were driven from their residences in Tripoli to the airport. Under the watchful eyes of UN officials and representatives from mediating nations like South Africa and Saudi Arabia, they boarded an aircraft. After a flight, likely involving a stopover, they landed at Valkenburg naval air base in the Netherlands. Awaiting them was a carefully choreographed security operation. They were escorted under heavy guard to Camp Zeist. There, within the newly designated Scottish territory, in a small, functional building prepared for the purpose, the formal handover took place.

Libyan officials transferred custody to UN representatives, who immediately transferred custody to waiting senior Scottish police officers. Megrahi and Fhimah were formally arrested under the Scottish warrants issued in 1991, informed of the charges against them, and processed into secure detention within the Camp Zeist complex. This quiet, legally precise procedure marked the dramatic end of the long international standoff. News of the handover flashed around the world. In New York, the UN Security Council immediately convened and passed Resolution 1192, formally confirming the suspension of the comprehensive sanctions imposed on Libya under Resolutions 748 and 883. While the sanctions were only suspended, not permanently lifted (pending the outcome of the trial and resolution of compensation issues), their suspension marked a major victory for Libya and the culmination of the diplomatic process. For the victims' families, it was a moment of profound significance – the suspects were finally in custody and would face trial. The unprecedented deal, born of tragedy, deadlock, and diplomacy, had delivered the accused. The focus now shifted entirely to the courtroom built on Dutch soil, where the long-delayed pursuit of justice in the Lockerbie bombing case was about to begin.

Chapter 9: The Case for the Prosecution

The third of May, 2000, dawned with a palpable sense of anticipation over the unique judicial enclave carved out within Camp Zeist, Netherlands. After years suspended in diplomatic limbo, the Lockerbie bombing case was finally entering a courtroom. The sheer novelty of the setting – a Scottish High Court convened on Dutch soil – underscored the extraordinary lengths taken to bring the two accused Libyans, Abdelbaset Ali Mohmed al-Megrahi and Lamin Khalifah Fhimah, to trial. Security was exceptionally tight; layers of checks by Dutch military police and Scottish constables guarded the perimeter and the entrance to the purpose-built courthouse, a modern, functional building standing in stark contrast to the historic stone courts of Edinburgh.

Inside, the atmosphere was thick with suppressed tension. Global media filled the designated press gallery, their presence testament to the intense international interest. Representatives from victims' families, having travelled from the UK, US, and beyond, occupied another section, their faces etched with a mixture of hope, anxiety, and the enduring pain of loss. UN observers, diplomats, and legal scholars were also present, ready to witness this unprecedented legal process unfold. In the dock sat the two accused, flanked by security officers, listening through headphones to the simultaneous Arabic translation. Facing them were their respective defence teams, led by some of Scotland's most prominent Queen's Counsel.

And presiding over all, on the elevated bench, were the three robed High Court judges – Lord Sutherland (initially, before illness led to Lord Cullen taking the chair), Lord Coulsfield, and Lord MacLean – upon whose shoulders rested the immense burden of discerning truth from the complex web of evidence to be presented over the coming months, without the assistance or buffer of a jury. As Lord Sutherland formally opened the proceedings, a profound silence settled. The moment of justice, however complex and delayed, had finally arrived. The prosecution, led by the Lord Advocate, Colin Boyd QC, rose to begin outlining the Crown's case – a narrative of meticulous planning, state-sponsored terrorism, and exploited vulnerabilities that aimed to trace the deadly trajectory of a single suitcase from a small Mediterranean island to the skies above Lockerbie.

The Suitcase Journey: Luggage Trails and Security Lapses

Lord Advocate Boyd's opening address, delivered over several hours, was a masterclass in legal exposition, designed to provide the judges with a comprehensive roadmap of the evidence the Crown intended to lead. He began by solemnly acknowledging the scale of the tragedy – the 270 lives lost, the devastation inflicted upon Lockerbie – before asserting the Crown's central contention: that this was no accident, but a deliberate act of mass murder, planned and executed by agents of the Libyan state, specifically the two men sitting in the dock. He outlined the prosecution's theory, detailing the alleged conspiracy: the acquisition of materials, the construction of the bomb concealed within a Toshiba radio cassette player packed inside a Samsonite suitcase with clothing purchased in Malta, the infiltration of this device into the international baggage system at Luqa Airport allegedly facilitated by Fhimah, its journey via Air Malta to Frankfurt, its transfer to the Pan Am feeder flight to Heathrow, and its final loading onto Pan Am 103, where it detonated precisely as intended. Boyd emphasized that the Crown's case would be built upon converging lines of evidence – sophisticated forensic science identifying the bomb and its components, detailed analysis of airline and airport procedures revealing critical security lapses, witness testimony placing the accused at key locations, and intelligence assessments pointing towards Libyan state involvement. It was, he promised, a circumstantial case in large part, but one where the accumulation of interconnected facts would point inexorably towards the guilt of both Megrahi and Fhimah.

The first major phase of the prosecution's evidence focused meticulously on reconstructing the alleged journey of the bomb suitcase, aiming to demonstrate not only that such a journey was possible, but that specific security failures at each stage were exploited. The narrative began at Luqa Airport, Malta, on the morning of December 21, 1988. The Crown called a series of witnesses who worked at Luqa: Air Malta baggage handlers described the process of sorting and loading luggage onto Flight KM180 bound for Frankfurt; check-in agents outlined procedures for accepting passenger bags; security personnel detailed the screening protocols (or lack thereof) in place for checked baggage at that time. Through careful questioning, the prosecution sought to establish the potential vulnerabilities in the system. Could an unaccompanied bag – one without a corresponding passenger travelling on the same flight – be introduced into the system, perhaps by someone with airside access? While witnesses often testified to standard procedures intended to prevent this, the prosecution elicited testimony suggesting that enforcement could be inconsistent, particularly for interline baggage tagged for onward destinations, and that someone with the authority and access of the LAA station manager might potentially circumvent checks. Documentary evidence, including Air Malta baggage handling manuals from 1988 and airport security directives, was presented. The Crown then focused specifically on Lamin Fhimah. Evidence was led confirming his role as LAA station manager, detailing his duties, responsibilities, and crucially, his possession of an airside pass granting access to all operational areas, including baggage sorting and loading ramps. Witness testimony was presented regarding Fhimah's presence and activities at Luqa Airport on the morning of December 21st. While no witness claimed to have seen Fhimah physically place the specific bomb suitcase onto the KM180 conveyor belt, the prosecution argued that his position provided the crucial opportunity, and his alleged affiliation with Libyan intelligence (evidence for which might be led later or inferred) provided the motive, to facilitate the introduction of the unaccompanied bag containing the bomb onto its first flight leg.

The next stage detailed the suitcase's arrival and transfer at Frankfurt Airport. Flight KM180 landed, and its baggage, including the interline bags destined for Pan Am flights, was unloaded and transferred to the Pan Am handling area in Terminal B. The prosecution called former Pan Am ground staff and Frankfurt Airport employees to testify about the procedures in place for handling and screening transit baggage in December 1988. Evidence was presented suggesting that Pan Am's X-ray screening at Frankfurt primarily focused on originating baggage, with inconsistent or potentially non-existent screening applied to interline bags arriving from other carriers like Air Malta, especially those destined for feeder flights like PA103A. The complexities of the baggage sorting system within the vast Frankfurt hub were detailed, highlighting potential points where a bag could bypass checks. Testimony emphasized the intense time pressures involved in transferring hundreds of bags between connecting flights, increasing the risk of procedural errors or shortcuts. Furthermore, the prosecution highlighted the apparent failure of Pan Am staff at Frankfurt to perform rigorous passenger-baggage reconciliation for the bags being loaded onto PA103A. They argued that the unaccompanied status of the bomb suitcase should have been detected at this stage if proper procedures had been followed, but systemic weaknesses allowed it to proceed, undetected, onto the Boeing 727 bound for London Heathrow.

The final leg of the journey involved the transfer at Heathrow, Pan Am's major European hub. When PA103A arrived from Frankfurt, its cargo of connecting baggage, including the lethal Samsonite, was unloaded and transported across the tarmac to the waiting 'Maid of the Seas' at Terminal 3. The prosecution presented testimony from Heathrow-based Pan Am baggage handlers, ramp agents, and loading supervisors responsible for PA103 that evening. They described the process of sorting bags arriving from the feeder flight and integrating them with the much larger volume of luggage checked in by passengers originating in London. The Crown meticulously questioned witnesses about the baggage reconciliation procedures employed by Pan Am at Heathrow for interline transit bags in 1988.

Evidence emerged suggesting that while originating bags were subject to some reconciliation efforts, transit bags arriving on feeder flights like PA103A often were not subjected to a final, rigorous check to ensure a corresponding passenger was actually boarding PA103. The prosecution argued this represented the final critical security failure. The unaccompanied bomb suitcase, having successfully passed through Luqa and Frankfurt, was loaded into baggage container AVE 4041 PA along with other Frankfurt-originating luggage. This container, investigators testified, was subsequently loaded into position 14L in the forward cargo hold of the Boeing 747. The prosecution used detailed airport diagrams, baggage handling flowcharts, and potentially computer simulations to illustrate this complex three-stage journey for the judges, repeatedly emphasizing the specific security loopholes at each airport – lack of rigorous screening for interline bags, failure of positive passenger-baggage reconciliation – which, they contended, were not merely unfortunate oversights but known vulnerabilities deliberately exploited by individuals with knowledge of the system, namely the accused.

Star Witness: Tony Gauci and the Clothing Purchase

Having meticulously traced the alleged physical path of the bomb suitcase from Malta to Pan Am 103's cargo hold, the prosecution shifted focus to forging the direct human link between the device and the accused. This involved presenting the crucial evidence connecting the suitcase's contents back to the island of Malta and, specifically, to Abdelbaset al-Megrahi. The groundwork was laid by forensic scientists who testified about the recovery of the blast-damaged Samsonite suitcase fragments and, critically, the microscopic clothing fibres found embedded within them. Detailed scientific reports were entered as evidence, outlining the complex process of fibre analysis – microscopy, comparison of dye signatures using techniques like thin-layer chromatography – which allowed the identification of the specific garments: the Yorkie tweed jacket, the C&A cardigan, the Levi's trousers, the Babygro sleepsuit, and others. Further testimony detailed the extensive international investigation undertaken to trace the manufacturing and retail distribution of these items, culminating in the remarkable finding that the only known retail outlet in the world to have sold that specific combination of garments from relevant manufacturing batches was Mary's House boutique in Sliema, Malta.

This chain of forensic evidence, the prosecution argued, irrefutably linked the bomb suitcase to this single shop. The stage was thus set for the appearance of the shop's owner, Tony Gauci. His arrival in the witness box at Camp Zeist was a moment of considerable courtroom drama. Presented by the Crown as a crucial eyewitness, Gauci, a Maltese national appearing somewhat overwhelmed by the formal, high-security environment, began his testimony, often speaking through an interpreter. Under careful questioning from the prosecution during his examination-in-chief, he recounted his memory of a specific sales transaction that had lodged in his mind due to its unusual nature. He described a male customer entering Mary's House and purchasing a range of clothing, predominantly menswear, but including the out-of-place item of a baby's sleepsuit. Gauci provided a description of the customer – recalling his approximate age (around 50), his physical build, and stating that he appeared, to Gauci, to be Libyan. He recalled the customer paying in cash and showing little interest in the specific sizes of the garments, suggesting they were perhaps not for his own use. One detail Gauci recalled vividly was that it was raining heavily outside, leading the customer to also purchase an umbrella. The prosecution then introduced meteorological records for Malta covering late November and early December 1988.

These records showed various days with rainfall, but the prosecution argued strongly that only one date – Wednesday, December 7th, 1988 – perfectly matched Gauci's recollection of heavy rain occurring during his shop's opening hours and within the timeframe consistent with other evidence (like Megrahi's known travel periods). Establishing this specific date was vital for the Crown's timeline, aiming to place Megrahi physically in Malta making this purchase just two weeks before the bombing. The climax of Gauci's direct evidence came with the in-court identification. After recounting the purchase and describing the customer, the lead prosecutor asked Gauci if he could see the man he served that day anywhere in the courtroom. All eyes turned towards the dock where Megrahi and Fhimah sat.

After a pause, during which he carefully scanned the faces before him, Gauci gestured towards Abdelbaset al-Megrahi, confirming he was the man who had bought the clothes. This electrifying moment provided the prosecution with apparently powerful, direct evidence linking Megrahi to items packed within the bomb suitcase. It was a connection that moved beyond scientific inference and relied on human recognition and memory.

The prosecution worked diligently to bolster the credibility of Gauci's testimony and link it to other strands of their case. They reintroduced the forensic evidence confirming the clothing fragments found in the wreckage originated from items sold at his shop. They presented complex travel records, including flight manifests and immigration documents, allegedly demonstrating that Megrahi had travelled to Malta, potentially using the alias 'Ahmed Khalifa Abdusamad', on dates encompassing December 7th, 1988. They highlighted Gauci's apparent consistency on the core details of the transaction across multiple interviews conducted years apart, portraying him as a reliable witness whose memory of an unusual sale remained clear. The prosecution argued that the purchase of the baby-gro, seemingly inexplicable for a man buying menswear, could be understood as part of the bomb-maker's tradecraft – perhaps intended as padding within the suitcase or to help disguise the shape of the device inside.

They addressed anticipated defence criticisms preemptively, suggesting that any minor inconsistencies in Gauci's recollections were natural given the passage of over a decade, and vouching for the fairness of the pre-trial identification procedures where Gauci had also picked out Megrahi's photograph (while downplaying or offering explanations for the acknowledged fact that Gauci had seen Megrahi's picture in the media prior to one key identification session). The Crown presented Tony Gauci as an honest citizen, caught up in extraordinary events, whose testimony, when viewed alongside the corroborating forensic and travel evidence, provided compelling proof of Megrahi's presence in Malta and his direct involvement in the preparations for the Lockerbie bombing. His evidence formed the critical bridge between the technical analysis of the bomb and the alleged actions of one of the accused, becoming a central battleground upon which much of the trial would turn. The prosecution concluded this phase believing they had successfully traced the bomb from its container back to the hands of their prime suspect.

Chapter 10: The Defence Responds

As the prosecution case, meticulously assembled over months of testimony and the presentation of thousands of documents and forensic exhibits, finally drew to a close, the unique courtroom at Camp Zeist braced for the inevitable counter-offensive. The burden of proof, as underscored repeatedly by legal principle and the presiding judges, remained squarely on the Crown to establish the guilt of Abdelbaset al-Megrahi and Lamin Khalifah Fhimah beyond reasonable doubt. The defence teams, led by Queen's Counsel William Taylor for Megrahi and Richard Keen for Fhimah, were under no obligation to prove their clients' innocence or even to present an alternative definitive narrative of events. Their singular goal was to dissect the Crown's case, expose its weaknesses, challenge its assumptions, and demonstrate that the evidence presented, however voluminous, failed to meet the demanding standard required for conviction under Scottish law. This involved a multi-faceted strategy: rigorously attacking the credibility of key prosecution witnesses, questioning the certainty of the forensic science, highlighting inconsistencies and gaps in the alleged chain of events, and, significantly, suggesting that the entire investigation might have been fundamentally flawed, potentially overlooking more plausible culprits in its alleged predetermined focus on Libya. The defence response unfolded over subsequent months, transforming the trial into a complex legal battleground where every crucial piece of evidence was subjected to intense scrutiny and challenge.

Attacking the Evidence: Timers, Testimony, and Doubt

The defence strategy began with a direct assault on the pillars supporting the Crown's case, aiming to crumble the foundations upon which the allegations rested. Unsurprisingly, the testimony of the Maltese shopkeeper, Tony Gauci, became a primary target, particularly for Megrahi's defence team led by William Taylor QC. During a protracted and often grueling cross-examination, Taylor painstakingly took Gauci back through his numerous statements given to Scottish police, FBI agents, and Maltese authorities since 1989. He highlighted, point by point, alleged discrepancies and evolutions in Gauci's account. These included variations in his initial description of the customer's height, build, age, and even clothing; shifts in his recollection of the precise date of the purchase (initially expressing uncertainty across several weeks before later settling more firmly on dates aligning with Megrahi's alleged presence); and inconsistencies regarding the exact items of clothing purchased compared to those forensically recovered. Taylor suggested that Gauci's memory was demonstrably fallible, potentially influenced by repeated questioning over many years, and possibly reconstructed, consciously or subconsciously, to fit the emerging narrative presented by investigators.

The defence reserved its most intense attack for the circumstances surrounding Gauci's identification of Megrahi. Taylor meticulously documented the timeline, emphasizing that Gauci failed to pick out Megrahi from photographic arrays shown to him on several occasions before he saw Megrahi's picture published in connection with the Lockerbie bombing in the international press.

The defence argued forcefully that this exposure created an irredeemable bias, planting Megrahi's image in Gauci's mind and rendering any subsequent identification unreliable. They dissected the procedures used during the critical September 1989 photo-spread session where Gauci eventually did identify Megrahi, questioning whether the array was properly constituted and whether subtle cues might have influenced the witness. The in-court identification at Camp Zeist, while dramatic, was portrayed by the defence as worthless, tainted by the prior exposure and suggestive influences. Furthermore, the defence aggressively pursued the issue of potential financial motivation. They cross-examined Gauci relentlessly about his awareness of the multi-million dollar reward offered by the US government for information leading to the Lockerbie bombers' conviction. While Gauci consistently denied that the reward influenced his testimony, the defence sought to persuade the judges that the sheer scale of the potential payout cast a significant shadow over his credibility and impartiality.

They argued that Gauci, facing potential financial gain, had a vested interest in providing testimony that aligned with the prosecution's desired narrative. The cumulative effect of this cross-examination strategy was designed to portray Tony Gauci not as the simple, honest witness the Crown depicted, but as someone whose memory was demonstrably unreliable, whose identification was fatally compromised by external suggestion, and whose motives were potentially clouded by the prospect of financial reward, thereby rendering his crucial evidence unsafe to found a conviction upon.

The defence launched an equally vigorous challenge against the forensic evidence derived from the MST-13 timer fragment, seeking to undermine its purported status as an exclusive link to Libya. Edwin Bollier, the co-founder of the Swiss manufacturer MEBO AG, endured lengthy and challenging cross-examination from defence counsel. Lawyers explored in minute detail the business practices, record-keeping, and security protocols (or lack thereof) at MEBO's Zurich facility. Bollier made several damaging admissions under questioning: he acknowledged that MEBO's security was not foolproof and that components, including potentially completed timers or circuit boards, could conceivably have been stolen or removed without authorization; he testified about modifications made to timers for different clients, raising questions about whether the fragment found truly matched only the specifications of the batch delivered to Libya; he conceded that MEBO had dealings with various state agencies, including potentially East German intelligence (the Stasi), creating ambiguity about who else might have had access to similar technology or expertise.

Defence lawyers meticulously dissected MEBO's invoices and technical documentation, arguing that the records were not sufficiently precise or complete to definitively prove that only Libya received timers with the exact characteristics of the recovered fragment. They highlighted inconsistencies in Bollier's own accounts given over the years regarding his dealings with Libyan officials, including Megrahi himself, attempting to portray him as an unreliable businessman perhaps tailoring his story to suit investigators or protect his own interests.

Furthermore, the defence likely called upon their own forensic electronics experts to testify, potentially questioning the methodology used by Crown experts to identify the fragment, suggesting alternative possible sources for such a tiny piece of circuit board, or emphasizing the difficulty of making a conclusive match from such limited material, especially after the violence of the explosion and subsequent environmental exposure. The defence also likely raised questions about the chain of custody of the fragment itself – discovered months after the crash, potentially amidst contaminated debris – arguing that its provenance could not be established beyond reasonable doubt. The objective was to neutralize the timer evidence, transforming it from the prosecution's 'golden thread' into just another ambiguous fragment incapable of definitively proving Libyan state responsibility or Megrahi's involvement.

The prosecution's carefully constructed narrative of the bomb suitcase's journey via Malta, Frankfurt, and Heathrow was also systematically deconstructed by the defence teams. Richard Keen QC, representing Lamin Fhimah, focused on demolishing the case against his client. He emphasized the complete lack of any direct evidence placing Fhimah in physical contact with the bomb suitcase or demonstrating his knowing participation in a conspiracy. He argued that Fhimah's presence and actions at Luqa Airport on December 21st were entirely consistent with his routine duties as LAA station manager. Keen likely presented witnesses – perhaps Fhimah's colleagues or other airport staff – to corroborate Fhimah's normal work patterns and to testify that they saw nothing suspicious in his behaviour. He challenged the prosecution's reliance on inference, arguing that opportunity afforded by Fhimah's airside pass did not constitute proof of criminal action.

He stressed the absence of any evidence of communication or coordination between Fhimah and Megrahi related to the alleged plot, portraying them simply as LAA colleagues. Fhimah's defence likely presented evidence of his character and lack of any prior involvement in illicit activities, arguing there was no credible motive for him to participate in such a horrific act. The core argument was that the Crown's case against Fhimah was built entirely on speculation and association, falling far short of the standard required for conviction.

Both defence teams vigorously challenged the prosecution's depiction of airport security in 1988 as universally lax and easily exploitable. Through cross-examination of airline and airport security personnel called by the Crown, and potentially by calling their own expert witnesses in aviation security, the defence sought to establish that procedures, while different from modern standards, did exist and were generally followed. They questioned the prosecution's assumptions about the ease with which an unaccompanied bag could pass through three international airports undetected. They highlighted specific checkpoints or procedures that should have identified such a bag if correctly implemented, suggesting that the prosecution's scenario required not just isolated lapses but potentially a series of unlikely failures or even deliberate collusion beyond the two accused. They probed for alternative explanations for any documented irregularities in baggage handling on the relevant days. Crucially, they hammered home the point that despite the recovery of tons of wreckage and thousands of personal items, not a single piece of direct forensic evidence – no fingerprint, no hair, no DNA – linked either Megrahi or Fhimah to the Samsonite suitcase, the Toshiba radio, the Semtex, the timer, or the clothing purchased by the mystery man in Malta. The entire edifice constructed by the prosecution regarding the suitcase journey, the defence argued, rested on a foundation of circumstantial inference, assumption, and contested witness testimony, lacking the concrete proof necessary to convict. They might also have raised specific technical forensic challenges, perhaps questioning the certainty of the Semtex identification methods used, exploring potential sources of contamination during the complex recovery and analysis process, or even challenging the statistical basis of the claim that Mary's House was the sole possible source for the specific clothing combination, suggesting flaws in the exhaustive tracing process. Every link in the prosecution's chain was tested, stretched, and declared insufficient to bear the weight of proof beyond reasonable doubt.

Alternative Theories Presented: Who Else Could Be Responsible?

Complementing the direct assault on the Crown's evidence was the defence strategy of actively presenting alternative scenarios for the bombing, designed to persuade the judges that reasonable doubt existed regarding Libya's sole responsibility. This involved revisiting and amplifying the theory that the bombing was orchestrated by the PFLP-GC, potentially funded by Iran and facilitated by Syria, as revenge for the downing of Iran Air 655. Defence counsel dedicated significant courtroom time to exploring this hypothesis. They cross-examined prosecution intelligence witnesses extensively, challenging the official narrative that this theory had been thoroughly investigated and definitively ruled out. They sought admissions about the known capabilities of the PFLP-GC, particularly their expertise in constructing barometric bombs concealed within Toshiba radios, citing the bombs seized during the 'Autumn Leaves' operation in Germany in October 1988 as concrete examples. They introduced evidence, perhaps through defence witnesses or by cross-referencing intelligence documents acknowledged by the Crown, detailing the PFLP-GC's presence and activities in Europe, their known links to Iranian and Syrian intelligence services, and the powerful motive provided by the Iran Air tragedy.

Defence lawyers meticulously compared the known components and design features of the PFLP-GC bombs seized in Germany with the device believed to have destroyed Pan Am 103, arguing that the similarities were striking and perhaps more significant than any differences highlighted by the prosecution.

They questioned why key figures associated with the PFLP-GC cell arrested in Germany, such as Hafez Dalkamoni or Marwan Khreesat (a Jordanian bomb-maker allegedly working with the group), were not pursued more vigorously as Lockerbie suspects. They suggested that crucial evidence pointing towards this alternative axis might have been ignored, suppressed, or conveniently lost by Western intelligence agencies, perhaps due to shifting geopolitical priorities, such as the need for Syrian cooperation during the First Gulf War which occurred shortly after the Lockerbie investigation gained momentum. The defence strongly implied that the intense focus on Libya might have been politically expedient, allowing Western governments to target a known adversary while potentially overlooking or downplaying evidence that implicated states like Iran or Syria, with whom relations were perhaps more complex or strategically sensitive at different times. They argued that the existence of this credible alternative scenario, involving actors with proven capability and motive, inherently created reasonable doubt about the prosecution's insistence on exclusive Libyan guilt.

Beyond the specific PFLP-GC/Iran/Syria theory, the defence broadly attacked the integrity and objectivity of the entire Operation Hornbeam investigation. They argued that investigators, faced with immense public and political pressure to solve the case, may have developed tunnel vision, latching onto the Libyan hypothesis early on (perhaps influenced by the timer fragment discovery) and subsequently interpreting all other evidence through that potentially biased lens. They questioned the handling of key witnesses like Gauci and Bollier, suggesting investigators may have unintentionally or even intentionally steered their testimony towards implicating the Libyans.

They highlighted any perceived procedural irregularities, gaps in the evidence chain, or failures to pursue potentially fruitful lines of inquiry that pointed away from Libya. The defence sought to portray the investigation not as an impartial search for truth, but as an exercise potentially marred by confirmation bias and perhaps even political manipulation, thereby undermining the reliability of its conclusions.

Furthermore, the defence explored other hypothetical vulnerabilities in the aviation security system of 1988 that could have allowed a bomb onto Pan Am 103, unrelated to the complex Malta-Frankfurt-Heathrow journey alleged by the Crown. They devoted considerable attention to security procedures at Heathrow Airport itself, the flight's point of departure for its transatlantic leg. Through cross-examination of Heathrow security managers, airline staff, and potentially independent security experts called as defence witnesses, they probed for weaknesses in passenger screening, cabin baggage checks, cargo security, catering supplies, and crucially, employee access controls and background checks. Could an insider at Heathrow, perhaps bribed or coerced, have placed a device on board? Were checks on airport staff entering secure areas sufficiently rigorous? Could the bomb have been introduced via cargo or mail rather than passenger baggage? While the defence likely lacked direct evidence to support a specific Heathrow-based plot, their aim was to demonstrate that multiple potential security breaches existed, and the Crown's focus on the convoluted Malta route, heavily reliant on circumstantial links and contested testimony, was not the only possibility, nor necessarily the most plausible one. By highlighting these alternative vulnerabilities, they further sought to dilute the certainty of the prosecution's case.

In essence, the defence narrative presented to the Camp Zeist judges was a comprehensive rebuttal. It argued that the Crown's case against Fhimah was almost entirely speculative, lacking any direct evidence of his involvement. Against Megrahi, they contended the key pillars were fatally flawed: Gauci's identification was unreliable and tainted; the timer fragment link to Libya was not proven to be exclusive beyond reasonable doubt; the alleged suitcase journey relied on a chain of assumptions and inferences rather than concrete proof; and no direct forensic evidence connected Megrahi to the bomb or its components. Compounding these alleged weaknesses, the defence presented a plausible, documented alternative theory involving the PFLP-GC, Iran, and Syria, which they argued the investigation had improperly dismissed. They suggested the entire investigation may have suffered from bias and procedural flaws. Cumulatively, the defence argued, these factors created far more than just theoretical possibilities; they established concrete, substantial reasons to doubt the prosecution's narrative. Under the exacting standard of Scottish criminal law, requiring proof beyond reasonable doubt, the defence teams concluded their presentation by asserting that the Crown had fundamentally failed to meet its burden, and therefore, both Abdelbaset al-Megrahi and Lamin Khalifah Fhimah were entitled to acquittal. The judges were left to deliberate upon a vast sea of conflicting evidence, forensic complexities, contested testimony, and competing narratives of international intrigue.

\

Chapter 11: The Verdict at Camp Zeist

The final days of January 2001 saw an almost unbearable tension gather around the starkly functional, high-security enclave of Camp Zeist. Inside the Scottish High Court building, convened extraordinarily on Dutch soil, the protracted legal battle over the Lockerbie bombing had concluded. Eighty-four days of complex evidence, spanning forensic science, international travel, witness testimony, and intelligence assessments, had been presented and rigorously challenged. The prosecution, marshalled by Lord Advocate Colin Boyd QC, had painstakingly constructed its case, alleging a Libyan state-sponsored plot executed by the two men in the dock, Abdelbaset al-Megrahi and Lamin Khalifah Fhimah. The defence teams, led by William Taylor QC and Richard Keen QC respectively, had mounted a formidable rebuttal, dissecting the Crown's evidence, attacking the credibility of key witnesses, and raising the spectre of alternative perpetrators. Following powerful closing submissions where each side forcefully argued their interpretation of the evidence and the law, the three presiding judges – Lord Cullen, Lord MacLean, and Lord Coulsfield – had retired to undertake their solemn, Herculean task: to deliberate upon the vast sea of conflicting information and, according to the stringent requirements of Scots law, reach a unanimous verdict on charges of conspiracy and the murder of 270 people.

Weeks passed as the judges meticulously reviewed transcripts, examined thousands of documents and exhibits, and debated the legal nuances. Outside the courtroom walls, speculation mounted, diplomats held their breath, and the families of the Pan Am 103 victims waited, suspended between hope for accountability and fear of further disappointment after more than twelve years of agonizing uncertainty. Finally, on the last day of January, word came: the judges were ready.

Guilty: The Judges' Decision on Megrahi

January 31, 2001. The courtroom at Camp Zeist was filled to capacity, the atmosphere electric with anticipation. Security personnel stood alert as the three judges filed in solemnly and took their places on the bench. In the dock, Megrahi and Fhimah, dressed in suits, appeared outwardly calm but the strain was palpable. The galleries were packed – family members leaning forward, journalists poised with notebooks, lawyers observing intently. Lord Cullen, the presiding judge, began to speak, his measured tones cutting through the silence. He announced that the court had reached its verdicts and proceeded to read from the comprehensive written opinion they had collectively authored, a document that would run to over 80 pages, detailing their exhaustive analysis of the evidence. As he addressed the charges against the first accused, Abdelbaset Ali Mohmed al-Megrahi, the tension became almost physical. Then came the words that reverberated around the world: "The verdict of the court is that the first accused, Abdelbaset Ali Mohmed al-Megrahi, is guilty of the crime of murder." Gasps, quickly stifled sobs, and a wave of intense, complex emotion swept through the public gallery.

Megrahi himself reportedly showed little reaction, listening impassively as the judgment confirming his conviction for orchestrating the deadliest terrorist attack in British history was delivered. The judges' decision to convict Megrahi was grounded entirely in their assessment of the circumstantial evidence, finding that the cumulative weight of interconnected facts and the inferences drawn therefrom were sufficient to meet the demanding standard of proof beyond reasonable doubt. Their lengthy written opinion provided a forensic dissection of the evidence they accepted and the reasoning behind their conclusions. Regarding the crucial MEBO MST-13 timer fragment, the judges explicitly addressed the defence challenges but ultimately accepted the Crown's position. They stated: "We accept that the fragment came from the board of an MST-13 timer, and that this timer was one of a number supplied by MEBO to Libya."

They acknowledged Edwin Bollier's sometimes "unsatisfactory" testimony and the theoretical possibility of timers going astray, but concluded: "On the whole matter, we are satisfied that it has been proved beyond reasonable doubt that the timer which initiated the explosion was one of those supplied by MEBO to Libya." They found the defence arguments about stolen timers or alternative sources lacked sufficient evidential basis to displace the strong inference from the exclusive supply contract. This finding provided the critical forensic link connecting the bomb's trigger mechanism directly to the Libyan state apparatus. Similarly, the judges accepted the forensic evidence tracing the clothing fragments recovered from the wreckage back to items sold exclusively at Mary's House in Malta. They found the scientific analysis compelling and the chain of investigation robust, stating the evidence "established beyond reasonable doubt" that the clothes packed in the primary suitcase originated from that specific shop. This finding then set the stage for their deeply considered assessment of Tony Gauci's testimony. The judges demonstrated a keen awareness of the significant weaknesses highlighted by the defence. They explicitly noted Gauci's inconsistencies regarding the date of purchase and the customer's description, remarking that his memory for detail appeared "poor". They devoted considerable attention to the controversial pre-trial identification, acknowledging that Gauci's exposure to Megrahi's photograph in the media "must cast doubt on the reliability of his identification". Indeed, they stated unequivocally: "It would be difficult, if not impossible, to hold that the identification by itself constituted proof beyond reasonable doubt that the first accused was the purchaser." However, they did not discard his evidence entirely. Under Scots law, corroboration is required for conviction, meaning one piece of evidence must be supported by independent evidence pointing towards the same conclusion. The judges found such corroboration existed for Gauci's identification, flawed though it was.

The corroborating evidence, in the judges' view, came primarily from the travel records allegedly placing Megrahi in Malta at the relevant time. They carefully analyzed flight manifests, immigration stamps, and hotel registration records (including one for the Holiday Inn in Sliema under the name 'Ahmed Khalifa Abdusamad', an alias the Crown attributed to Megrahi based on other evidence). They concluded: "It has been established that the first accused arrived in Malta by flight KM231 on 20 December 1988 and left Malta... on flight KM180 to Frankfurt on the morning of 21 December 1988... Further... there is evidence from which it may be inferred that the first accused was also in Malta on 7 December 1988," the date argued by the Crown as the most likely day for the clothing purchase based on Gauci's recollection of rain. The judges reasoned that Megrahi's proven presence in Malta on dates encompassing the likely purchase window provided the necessary independent corroboration required by law to support Gauci's identification, despite its inherent weaknesses. They stated: "Putting the matter shortly, the evidence of the identification, questionable though it was in some respects, was corroborated... by the evidence of the first accused's presence in Malta." They explicitly addressed the defence arguments about media contamination and potential financial reward, finding that while these were relevant considerations, they did not, in the context of the corroborating evidence, create a reasonable doubt about the core fact that Megrahi was the man who purchased the clothes.

Having accepted the timer link to Libya, the clothing link to Malta, and the corroborated identification placing Megrahi in Malta purchasing those clothes, the judges then drew the ultimate inference of guilt. They considered the sophisticated nature of the bomb and the plot, concluding it was clearly state-sponsored. They noted Megrahi's established position within Libyan intelligence (JSO/ESO) and his known connections to MEBO. They pieced together the circumstantial evidence: Megrahi had access to the specific type of timer used; he was present in Malta at the time the clothing packed around the bomb was purchased; he was identified (albeit imperfectly but corroborated) as the purchaser. The judges concluded that the convergence of these independent strands of evidence led to an "inescapable inference" that Megrahi played a central role in the conspiracy, specifically in obtaining the timer and preparing the primary suitcase containing the bomb in Malta.

They stated: "There is nothing in the evidence which leaves us with any reasonable doubt as to the guilt of the first accused." The conviction was thus secured, not on any single piece of irrefutable proof, but on the judges' acceptance of a powerful combination of interconnected circumstantial evidence, corroborated according to the requirements of Scots law.

A few days after the verdict, Megrahi faced sentencing. Lord Cullen, delivering the sentence, reiterated the horrific nature of the crime – the calculated mass murder of 270 innocent people. He imposed the mandatory sentence for murder in Scotland: imprisonment for life. Recognizing the gravity of the offence, the judges recommended a minimum period, or 'punishment part', of 20 years before Megrahi could be considered for parole. (This minimum term was subsequently appealed by the Crown as unduly lenient, and the High Court Appeal Bench later increased it substantially to 27 years, reflecting the exceptional barbarity of the crime). Following sentencing, Megrahi began his long imprisonment in Scotland, transferred from the unique setting of Camp Zeist to the realities of the Scottish prison system, albeit within a dedicated unit subject to UN monitoring as agreed in the pre-trial deal. The judicial process at Camp Zeist had delivered its verdict on him: Guilty.

Acquitted: The Fate of Lamin Fhimah and its Implications

The delivery of the verdict for the second accused, Lamin Khalifah Fhimah, followed immediately upon Megrahi's conviction, maintaining the palpable tension in the courtroom. As Lord Cullen addressed the charges against Fhimah, his conclusion stood in stark contrast: "As regards the second accused, Lamin Khalifah Fhimah, the verdict of the court is Not Guilty." A wave of relief washed over Fhimah, visible even through the formal courtroom setting. His defence team, led by Richard Keen QC, exchanged quiet congratulations. While the families in the gallery registered the decision with mixed, often muted, reactions, the acquittal of one defendant while the other was convicted immediately highlighted the nuanced and evidence-specific nature of the judges' deliberations.

The court's detailed written opinion provided a clear and compelling explanation for Fhimah's acquittal, resting squarely on the fundamental principle of the burden of proof. The judges concluded that the Crown had simply failed to present sufficient credible evidence to prove Fhimah's participation in the conspiracy beyond reasonable doubt. They acknowledged the prosecution's core argument: that Fhimah's position as LAA station manager at Luqa Airport, with his airside access and knowledge of procedures, provided him with the opportunity to introduce the unaccompanied bomb suitcase onto Air Malta Flight KM180. However, they drew a sharp distinction between opportunity and proof of criminal action.

The judges stated explicitly: "Proof that the second accused had the opportunity to assist in the introduction of the primary suitcase into the baggage system... is not sufficient of itself to satisfy us beyond reasonable doubt that he did so." The judgment meticulously dissected the evidence presented against Fhimah, finding it wanting in several key respects. Primarily, they emphasized the complete lack of any direct evidence linking him to the crime. No witness saw Fhimah handle the specific Samsonite suitcase or engage in any demonstrably illicit activity related to the loading of KM180 on December 21st. No forensic evidence connected him in any way to the bomb, the suitcase, its contents, or Megrahi's alleged activities in Malta. The Crown's case against him, the judges found, was built entirely on inference: inferring his guilt from his job, his access, and his association with Megrahi. The judges examined the evidence regarding Fhimah's actions and movements at Luqa Airport on the crucial morning. While confirming his presence and routine duties, they found nothing in his behaviour, as described by witnesses, that was necessarily inconsistent with his legitimate role as station manager. There was no evidence presented, for instance, of him overriding security procedures, acting furtively, or giving unusual instructions related to baggage handling for KM180.

Regarding the association between Fhimah and Megrahi, the judges acknowledged evidence confirming they knew each other, that Megrahi sometimes visited Fhimah's airport office during his trips to Malta, and that they might be considered friends or at least professional colleagues within the LAA/Libyan structure. However, the court found no evidence of communication or coordination between the two men specifically relating to the bombing plot.

Mere association, the judges reasoned, could not form the basis for inferring complicity in such a serious crime. They concluded that while the evidence might raise suspicion about Fhimah, particularly given his LAA role and Megrahi's conviction, suspicion alone is insufficient in law. The Crown had failed to eliminate reasonable doubt. The judgment stated: "While the association of the second accused with the first accused... and his position as station manager for LAA at the airport raise suspicion, there is no evidence which directly implicates the second accused in the conspiracy... The Crown case against him depended upon inference... We are of the opinion that the evidence... is not sufficient to overcome the presumption of innocence." Fhimah was acquitted because the evidence, in the court's unanimous view, did not meet the high standard required for a criminal conviction in Scotland.

Following the delivery of the not guilty verdict, Lamin Fhimah was formally discharged by the court. After nearly two years in custody at Camp Zeist, he walked out of the courthouse complex a free man. Arrangements were quickly made for his departure from the Netherlands. He flew back to Tripoli, where the Gaddafi regime orchestrated a triumphant homecoming. Fhimah was greeted by cheering crowds, hailed by state officials as a national hero who had withstood false accusations from hostile Western powers, and celebrated as living proof of Libya's innocence and the alleged political bias of the trial. His acquittal was heavily exploited for propaganda purposes, used by Libya to undermine the significance of Megrahi's conviction and bolster its long-standing claims of being unfairly targeted.

The split verdict inevitably generated complex and diverse reactions. The prosecution expressed satisfaction with Megrahi's conviction, viewing it as validation of their core case and a significant achievement in holding a state-sponsored terrorist accountable, while expressing disappointment but accepting the court's decision regarding Fhimah. Megrahi's defence team immediately confirmed their intention to appeal his conviction, citing the judges' acknowledged reliance on flawed identification evidence and contested forensic links. Fhimah's lawyers celebrated his acquittal as a just outcome reflecting the lack of evidence against him. For the victims' families, the split verdict brought a maelstrom of emotions. Many felt profound relief and a sense of partial justice achieved through Megrahi's conviction, seeing it as confirmation of Libyan guilt. Others expressed deep frustration and anger at Fhimah's acquittal, feeling that a key player had escaped justice or that the verdict somehow diminished the finding against Megrahi.

For some families who harboured doubts about the Libyan-centric investigation, Fhimah's acquittal perhaps reinforced their belief that the full truth remained hidden or that the case against Megrahi was weaker than claimed. The verdict did not unify the families but reflected their diverse perspectives and ongoing pain. Internationally, the US and UK governments formally respected the court's independence and accepted both verdicts, while carefully reiterating their position that the trial confirmed Libyan state involvement (through Megrahi's conviction) and maintaining pressure on Libya to formally accept responsibility and agree to comprehensive compensation for the families. Libya, conversely, used Fhimah's acquittal to claim vindication, while denouncing Megrahi's conviction as a miscarriage of justice driven by political motives.

The verdict at Camp Zeist, therefore, while providing legal finality at the trial stage for the two individuals accused, did not end the Lockerbie saga. It resolved the question of individual criminal liability for Megrahi and Fhimah under Scottish law, but it left the broader issues of state responsibility, compensation, and the persistent controversies surrounding the evidence and investigation very much alive, ensuring that the echoes of Pan Am 103 would continue to reverberate for years to come.

Chapter 12: The Prisoner of Greenock

The guilty verdict pronounced in the unique setting of the Scottish Court at Camp Zeist was, for Abdelbaset al-Megrahi, not an end but a transition. The culmination of the unprecedented trial phase marked the beginning of a new, stark reality: life imprisonment within the confines of the Scottish prison system. The carefully constructed judicial enclave in the Netherlands, with its specific protocols and international oversight focused on the trial process itself, gave way to the established routines, inherent restrictions, and complex social dynamics of conventional high-security incarceration. His transfer from Dutch soil back to Scotland in February 2001, mere days after being sentenced, symbolized this shift. While the legal battle was far from over, with his defence team immediately signalling their intent to appeal, Megrahi's physical existence was now defined by prison walls, locked doors, and the loss of liberty that accompanies a conviction for mass murder. Concurrently, the machinery of the Scottish legal system prepared for the next phase – the rigorous process of appellate review, where Megrahi's lawyers would seek to persuade a panel of senior judges that the trial court's verdict was flawed and constituted a miscarriage of justice. This chapter chronicles the dual realities of Megrahi's life in the years immediately following his conviction: the mundane yet challenging experience of long-term imprisonment in Scotland, and the commencement of his complex and determined legal fight for exoneration.

Life Sentence: Inside HMP Barlinnie and Greenock

The transfer of Abdelbaset al-Megrahi from Camp Zeist back to Scotland was executed with considerable security and discretion. Following the sentencing hearing where Lord Cullen imposed the mandatory life sentence and recommended a minimum term of 20 years, arrangements were swiftly made. Megrahi was likely transported under heavy police and prison service escort from Camp Zeist to a Dutch airfield, possibly the same Valkenburg naval base used for his arrival nearly two years prior. He would then have been flown on a dedicated, secure flight – perhaps a military or chartered aircraft – to an airport in Scotland, likely Glasgow or Prestwick, met by another substantial security detail for the final road transfer. His initial destination within the Scottish Prison Service (SPS) estate was HMP Barlinnie, located in the Riddrie area of Glasgow.

Barlinnie prison, opened in 1882, stands as one of Scotland's largest and most imposing penal institutions. A sprawling complex dominated by traditional Victorian prison architecture, it primarily serves the busy courts of Glasgow and the surrounding Strathclyde region, housing a diverse population of remand and convicted prisoners, often operating near or above its official capacity. Its reputation within Scotland is formidable, often associated with overcrowding, gang-related issues amongst inmates, and the inherent challenges of managing a large, complex prison population. Placing Megrahi, arguably the most high-profile and potentially vulnerable prisoner ever held in Scotland, into this environment required extraordinary measures. He was immediately assigned to a 'special unit' within Barlinnie, physically segregated from the main prison wings.

Such units are designed for prisoners requiring exceptional security management, either due to the nature of their offence, risks posed to them by other inmates, or risks they might pose themselves. Within this unit, Megrahi would have occupied a single cell, his movements heavily restricted, and his interactions limited to carefully vetted prison staff and possibly a very small number of other prisoners managed under similar conditions. His daily routine would have been rigidly structured: specified times for lock-up, meals (likely delivered to his cell initially), exercise (perhaps alone in a secure yard), and any approved activities. The contrast with the Camp Zeist environment, where he had relatively freer movement within the secure complex and daily contact with his extensive legal team, must have been profound and psychologically jarring.

As stipulated in the pre-trial agreements brokered by the UN, Megrahi's imprisonment in Scotland remained subject to international monitoring to ensure his treatment conformed to globally recognized standards for prisoners' rights. Representatives from the United Nations, likely designated observers, were granted periodic access to visit Megrahi, inspect his conditions of confinement, review his access to healthcare and legal representation, and report back to the UN Secretary-General. These monitoring arrangements provided an unusual layer of external scrutiny on the Scottish Prison Service's handling of its most famous inmate, ensuring compliance with the guarantees given to Libya as part of the deal securing the suspects' handover for trial. Reports from these observations generally indicated that while imprisoned under high security, Megrahi's basic rights were respected within the framework of the Scottish system.

After a period assessed within Barlinnie's challenging environment, Megrahi was transferred to HMP Greenock. Situated overlooking the Firth of Clyde, Greenock is a smaller prison than Barlinnie, historically housing a mix of local prisoners and longer-term inmates from across Scotland. Its transfer may have been prompted by operational considerations, perhaps offering a more stable, manageable long-term environment for a prisoner requiring permanent high-security segregation. While still operating under maximum security protocols, the regime at Greenock might have offered slightly different routines or facilities compared to the larger Glasgow prison. Regardless of the specific location, the core realities of Megrahi's incarceration remained constant. He was serving a life sentence for a crime of almost unimaginable horror, confined within a system far removed from his home, family, and culture.

Accounts from this period, often relayed through family members or lawyers, consistently portrayed him as maintaining his innocence with quiet determination. He reportedly immersed himself in studying, pursuing academic courses available through the prison education system, and spent countless hours poring over legal documents related to his case, actively participating in the preparation of his appeal. He adhered strictly to his Muslim faith, observing daily prayers within the constraints of the prison environment. Healthcare was provided through the standard SPS procedures, involving regular access to prison medical staff and escorted visits to external hospitals or specialists when required, always under strict security.

The emotional and logistical challenges for Megrahi's family were immense. His wife, Aisha, and their children remained in Libya. Visiting him in Scotland required obtaining visas, undertaking long and expensive international journeys (often complicated by the residual effects of sanctions or flight restrictions), and navigating the strict protocols of prison visits. These visits, occurring perhaps only a few times a year, took place in secure visiting areas, often with limited physical contact, under the watchful eyes of prison staff. They were undoubtedly moments of intense emotional significance for Megrahi and his family, providing vital human connection but also underscoring the painful reality of their separation. Throughout his imprisonment, Megrahi continued to receive substantial support from the Libyan state.

The Gaddafi regime, viewing his conviction as politically motivated and unjust, funded his extensive and costly legal defence and appeal efforts, employing top Scottish and international lawyers. Libyan consular officials maintained regular contact, monitoring his welfare and liaising with prison authorities. This state backing was crucial for sustaining his long legal battle. Within the broader context, Megrahi remained a figure of intense public fascination and division. To many, especially victims' families, he was the justly convicted perpetrator of mass murder. To a growing number of campaigners, journalists, and legal observers who questioned the evidence presented at Camp Zeist, he became the potential victim of a monumental miscarriage of justice. His life behind the walls of Greenock prison continued under this complex shadow of guilt, doubt, and international scrutiny.

Appeals and Reviews: The Fight for Exoneration Begins

The Scottish legal system provides an established, albeit complex, pathway for appealing criminal convictions handed down by the High Court of Justiciary. Immediately following Megrahi's conviction in January 2001 and sentencing in February 2001, his defence team lodged a formal Note of Appeal, signalling their intention to challenge the verdict before the High Court sitting in its appellate capacity as the Court of Criminal Appeal. This court, typically comprising three or five senior judges (including the Lord Justice-General or the Lord Justice Clerk, Scotland's two most senior judges), reviews convictions based on specific grounds. These generally include alleged errors in law made by the trial judge(s) in their directions or rulings, arguments that the verdict was unreasonable or unsupported by the evidence (a high threshold to meet, requiring the appeal court to find that no reasonable tribunal could have convicted on the evidence presented), or the emergence of significant fresh evidence that was not available, and could not reasonably have been made available, at the time of the trial.

The appeal is primarily a review of the original trial record and judgment; it is not a retrial where witnesses are re-examined, although new evidence can be heard in exceptional circumstances. Megrahi's appeal team, spearheaded again by William Taylor QC, spent months meticulously preparing the grounds of appeal, dissecting the trial judges' lengthy opinion and identifying areas where they believed fundamental errors had occurred.

The appeal hearing itself commenced in January 2002, reconvening remarkably within the same bespoke courtroom at Camp Zeist where the trial had taken place. This decision maintained legal consistency and addressed the ongoing security and logistical considerations. A panel of five appeal judges assembled, presided over by the Lord Justice-General, Lord Cullen, who, in a unique situation, was now leading the appellate review of a verdict delivered by a bench he himself had presided over at first instance (a situation permissible under the specific structure of the Scottish system at the time, though potentially raising questions of appearance).

The defence presented multiple, detailed grounds of appeal over several weeks of legal argument. A central plank, inevitably, was a renewed and legally focused attack on the trial judges' handling of the Tony Gauci identification evidence. The defence argued that the trial judges had fundamentally misapplied the Scottish law on corroboration. They contended that Gauci's identification of Megrahi was so inherently weak, unreliable, and demonstrably tainted by pre-trial media exposure that it could not, in law, be considered capable of being corroborated by other circumstantial evidence like Megrahi's presence in Malta. They cited legal precedents emphasizing that corroborated evidence must come from independent sources and argued that finding Megrahi was merely in Malta did not independently confirm he was the specific person in Gauci's shop. They argued the trial judges effectively used the flawed identification to interpret the travel evidence, rather than using independent travel evidence to corroborate the identification, allegedly reversing the proper legal test.

They submitted that accepting such flawed evidence as the basis for conviction rendered the verdict a miscarriage of justice.

Another major ground focused on the MEBO timer fragment evidence. The defence reiterated their challenges to the certainty of the forensic identification and, more forcefully, to the trial judges' acceptance of the evidence suggesting an exclusive supply of MST-13 timers to Libya. They dissected Edwin Bollier's trial testimony, highlighting his admissions about security issues, potential modifications, and dealings with other entities. They argued the judges failed to give adequate weight to these uncertainties and wrongly concluded that the Libyan link was established beyond reasonable doubt. They may have introduced further analysis or expert opinion challenging the exclusivity claim or the forensic interpretation of the fragment. The defence argued that without a definitively proven, exclusive link between the timer and Libya, this critical piece of circumstantial evidence crumbled, fatally weakening the inference of Megrahi's involvement. Further grounds likely included challenging the judges' interpretation of other circumstantial evidence, such as the travel records associated with the 'Abdusamad' alias, and potentially arguing that the Crown had failed to disclose relevant information during the trial (a common ground in miscarriage of justice claims). The core submission was that the trial judges had erred in their assessment of key evidence, misapplied legal principles regarding corroboration and reasonable doubt, and reached a verdict that was ultimately unreasonable and unsafe given the totality of the evidence and its inherent weaknesses.

The Crown, represented again by senior prosecutors from the Crown Office, mounted a robust defence of the original verdict and the trial judges' reasoning. They argued that the trial judges were fully entitled, based on the evidence presented, to find Gauci's core testimony credible despite its inconsistencies, and that his identification, while flawed, was legally capable of being corroborated by the independent evidence of Megrahi's presence in Malta at the relevant time. They submitted that the trial judges had correctly applied the established Scots law on corroboration in circumstantial cases. Regarding the timer, the Crown defended the trial court's finding, arguing that the judges had carefully considered Bollier's evidence and the defence challenges but were entitled to conclude, based on MEBO's records and other testimony, that the exclusive Libyan link was proven to the required standard. They emphasized that appellate courts should be reluctant to interfere with the trial court's assessment of witness credibility or its findings of fact unless they were demonstrably unreasonable or based on a clear error of law. The Crown maintained that the trial judges had meticulously evaluated all the evidence, correctly applied the law, and reached a verdict reasonably available to them based on the powerful convergence of multiple strands of circumstantial evidence pointing towards Megrahi's guilt.

After weeks of complex legal debate back in the familiar setting of Camp Zeist, the five appeal judges retired to deliberate. Their judgment, delivered on March 14, 2002, was unanimous and decisive: the appeal was refused. The appeal court, in another lengthy written opinion, systematically rejected each of the defence's grounds.

They endorsed the trial judges' approach to corroboration regarding the Gauci identification, finding no error in law in how they combined the identification evidence (despite its flaws) with the independent evidence of Megrahi's presence in Malta. They upheld the trial judges' assessment of the timer evidence, finding that the conclusion linking the fragment exclusively to the Libyan supply was one reasonably open to the trial court on the evidence presented. They found no merit in the other grounds of appeal relating to alleged non-disclosure or misinterpretation of evidence. The appeal judges concluded that the trial court had considered all the evidence fairly, applied the law correctly, and reached a verdict that was not unreasonable. Megrahi's conviction and life sentence were formally upheld by Scotland's highest criminal appeal court.

The failure of this first appeal represented a significant legal setback for Megrahi, seemingly closing the door on conventional routes for challenging his conviction within the Scottish judicial system. While the theoretical possibility of an application to the European Court of Human Rights in Strasbourg existed, focusing perhaps on fair trial arguments related to the identification procedure or evidence disclosure, the ECHR typically does not overturn domestic court findings of fact and success was far from guaranteed. However, the Scottish legal landscape now contained another important avenue: the Scottish Criminal Cases Review Commission (SCCRC). Established by an Act of Parliament in 1999, the SCCRC was created specifically to investigate potential miscarriages of justice after the normal appeal process has been exhausted.

Possessing significant investigative powers – including the ability to obtain police files, commission expert reports, and interview witnesses – the SCCRC could review convictions and, if it found compelling grounds to believe a miscarriage of justice might have occurred (such as significant new evidence or fundamental flaws in the original trial or appeal), it could refer the case back to the High Court for a fresh appeal. This offered a crucial potential lifeline. Megrahi's legal team and his growing number of supporters, including campaigners convinced of his innocence and sections of the media and legal academia questioning the safety of the conviction, immediately turned their attention towards preparing a detailed submission to the SCCRC. They began compiling new information, re-analyzing old evidence, and formulating arguments intended to persuade the Commission that Megrahi's case warranted reopening. The fight for exoneration, far from being extinguished by the appeal court's decision, was poised to enter a new, complex, and potentially lengthy phase, ensuring that the 'Prisoner of Greenock' remained at the centre of enduring legal and political controversy.

Chapter 13: The Compassionate Release

The rejection of Abdelbaset al-Megrahi's first appeal by the Scottish High Court in March 2002 appeared, to many observers, to mark the definitive legal endpoint in his challenge against the Lockerbie conviction. Yet, for Megrahi, continuing to serve his life sentence primarily within the secure confines of HMP Greenock, and for his dedicated legal team and supporters, the fight was far from over. The focus shifted towards a different, specialized legal avenue: the Scottish Criminal Cases Review Commission (SCCRC). Established in 1999 as an independent body tasked with investigating potential miscarriages of justice after the normal appeal process had been exhausted, the SCCRC offered a pathway, albeit a long and arduous one, to potentially reopen the case. Megrahi's lawyers began compiling a voluminous application, meticulously re-examining every facet of the original trial evidence, highlighting perceived flaws, inconsistencies, and importantly, seeking out new information that might cast doubt on the safety of the conviction.

This process consumed several years, involving detailed legal argument, forensic re-analysis, and potentially new witness interviews. Finally, in June 2007, the SCCRC delivered a significant decision: it concluded that there were indeed grounds upon which a miscarriage of justice might have occurred in Megrahi's case and formally referred his conviction back to the High Court for a second appeal.

The Commission identified six specific grounds for the referral, raising substantial questions about the non-disclosure of evidence by the Crown, uncertainties surrounding the timer fragment's provenance, and significant concerns regarding the reliability and credibility of Tony Gauci's crucial identification evidence. This referral was a major development, validating many of the doubts long expressed by critics of the verdict and setting the stage for a fresh, comprehensive judicial review of Megrahi's conviction. Preparations for this second, potentially explosive appeal commenced. However, before this complex legal process could reach its conclusion, dramatic developments concerning Megrahi's personal health intervened, irrevocably altering the course of events and triggering one of the most intense political and diplomatic controversies in modern Scottish and British history.

Terminal Diagnosis: The Compassionate Release Application

While the legal wheels turned slowly in preparation for the second appeal, Abdelbaset al-Megrahi's physical condition within HMP Greenock began a noticeable decline. Throughout his years of incarceration since 2001, he had received regular medical attention from the Scottish Prison Service (SPS) healthcare team for various ailments, as is standard procedure for all prisoners. However, during 2008, reports emerged suggesting more serious health concerns. Megrahi complained of increasing pain and other symptoms, leading to a series of diagnostic tests conducted both within the prison's medical facilities and at external NHS hospitals, always under secure escort.

These investigations culminated, likely in late 2008 or very early 2009, in a devastating diagnosis: Megrahi was suffering from advanced prostate cancer. Further tests confirmed the cancer was metastatic, meaning it had spread beyond the prostate gland, primarily to his bones. This stage of prostate cancer is generally considered incurable, with treatment focusing on managing symptoms and potentially extending lifespan, but not offering a cure.

A series of detailed medical assessments were conducted by NHS oncologists, urologists, and palliative care specialists contracted by the SPS to evaluate Megrahi's condition and prognosis. Their reports, submitted to the prison authorities and eventually forming the basis of legal applications, painted a grim picture. They confirmed the advanced, metastatic nature of the cancer and concluded it was terminal. Estimating life expectancy in such cases is notoriously difficult, varying significantly between individuals based on factors like the cancer's aggressiveness, response to treatment (such as hormone therapy), and overall health. However, the consensus among the various specialists consulted appeared to converge on a prognosis measured in months rather than years. The figure that became widely cited, and which formed the explicit basis for subsequent decisions, was a median life expectancy of approximately three months, although some reports may have indicated a slightly wider potential range. This dire medical situation brought into play specific provisions within Scottish law that allow for the early release of prisoners on compassionate grounds.

The legal authority for compassionate release resided solely with the Scottish Justice Secretary, a cabinet minister within the devolved Scottish Government in Edinburgh. The relevant legislation, principally the Prisons (Scotland) Act 1989 and related policy guidelines, empowered the Justice Secretary to order the release of any prisoner on licence if satisfied that "special circumstances exist which justify the prisoner's release on compassionate grounds." While the statute didn't explicitly define "special circumstances," long-standing practice and published Scottish Government guidelines focused primarily on cases involving prisoners suffering from a terminal illness with a short life expectancy. The commonly cited (though not legally binding) benchmark was a prognosis of three months or less, indicating the prisoner was likely nearing the end of life.

A second crucial element was an assessment that the prisoner's release would not pose an undue risk to public safety. Given the nature of Megrahi's crime, this assessment required careful consideration, but his severe illness likely mitigated concerns about future offending. Compassionate release is fundamentally an act of executive clemency, distinct from parole eligibility (which is determined by the Parole Board based on risk assessment after serving a minimum term) or judicial appeal (which addresses the safety of the conviction itself). It allows the Justice Secretary, based on compelling humanitarian circumstances related to a prisoner's terminal health, to grant release as an act of mercy, typically allowing the individual to die at home rather than in prison.

Acting upon the confirmed medical diagnosis and prognosis, Megrahi's legal team formally lodged an application for his release on compassionate grounds in the summer of 2009. The application, submitted directly to Justice Secretary Kenny MacAskill, presented the comprehensive medical reports from numerous consulting physicians detailing the advanced stage of the prostate cancer, its metastatic spread, the terminal prognosis, and the estimated short life expectancy. The legal submission argued that Megrahi's circumstances precisely matched the criteria set out in the legislation and established policy guidelines for compassionate release. It emphasized the humanitarian imperative, appealing to principles of mercy and dignity in allowing a terminally ill man, regardless of his conviction, to spend his final days with his family in his home country. Implicitly, the application also highlighted the practical benefits for the Scottish authorities of releasing Megrahi – relieving the SPS of the significant burden and expense of providing complex palliative care within a high-security prison setting, and removing a highly sensitive and resource-intensive prisoner from their custody.

The consideration of this application within the Scottish Government was complex and occurred alongside intense activity on two other related fronts. Megrahi's second appeal, following the SCCRC referral, was actively progressing through preliminary legal stages. Simultaneously, intense discussions were ongoing regarding a potential Prisoner Transfer Agreement (PTA) between the UK and Libya. A framework PTA had been signed, potentially allowing Megrahi (and other prisoners) to be transferred to serve the remainder of their sentence in their home country.

The PTA route required agreement between both governments and involved different criteria than compassionate release. These three tracks – compassionate release (a Scottish decision based on health), the second appeal (a judicial review of the conviction), and the PTA (a UK-Libyan governmental agreement) – became critically intertwined during July and August 2009. Intense lobbying occurred, with the Libyan government strongly advocating for Megrahi's return through either the PTA or compassionate release. Victims' families also made powerful representations, with many vehemently opposing any form of release, while a smaller number supported release on compassionate grounds or due to doubts about his conviction. A crucial, and highly controversial, development came just days before MacAskill's decision: Megrahi formally applied to abandon his second appeal.

His stated reason was his severe illness and desire to focus his remaining energy on returning home to die with his family. However, this move immediately fueled speculation among critics that dropping the appeal, which potentially could have overturned the conviction and caused significant embarrassment, was an implicit condition for securing his release through compassionate grounds or the PTA – an allegation consistently denied by both Megrahi's team and the Scottish Government. The Justice Secretary was thus faced with deciding on two parallel applications (compassionate release and PTA) while the potentially explosive second appeal was suddenly withdrawn, creating an extremely high-pressure political and legal environment.

Political Firestorm: Scotland, London, Washington, and Tripoli

On August 20, 2009, after weeks of intense speculation and behind-the-scenes deliberation, Kenny MacAskill convened a press conference at the Scottish Government's headquarters in St Andrew's House, Edinburgh. His announcement sent shockwaves around the globe. He confirmed he had decided to release Abdelbaset al-Megrahi from prison purely on compassionate grounds, effective immediately. Simultaneously, he announced he had rejected the separate application to transfer Megrahi to Libya under the PTA. In a detailed and carefully prepared statement, MacAskill explained his reasoning at length. He emphasized his statutory duty as Justice Secretary under Scots law to consider the compassionate release application based on the evidence presented.

He detailed the consistent medical advice he had received from multiple experts confirming Megrahi suffered from terminal, metastatic prostate cancer and had a prognosis measured in months, likely around three. He stated: "Mr. al-Megrahi is suffering from terminal prostate cancer... The medical advice from all the clinicians who have advised my officials and me is that he is now suffering from the final stages of his terminal illness... Clinical assessment is that he has a life expectancy of less than three months." Based on this medical evidence, MacAskill asserted, Megrahi clearly met the criteria for compassionate release established in law and policy. He framed his decision as one rooted in Scottish values, stating: "It is my decision that Mr Abdelbaset Ali Mohmed al-Megrahi, convicted in 2001 for the Lockerbie bombing, now terminally ill with prostate cancer, be released on compassionate grounds and allowed to return to

Libya to die... [1] *Our justice system demands that judgment be imposed, but compassion be available. Our beliefs dictate that justice be served, but mercy be shown.* [2] *Mr al-Megrahi now faces a sentence imposed by a higher power."* He took pains to stress that his decision was based solely on the medical evidence and the principles of compassion embedded within Scots law, explicitly denying it was influenced by any political pressure, diplomatic considerations, trade deals (specifically refuting any link to BP's oil interests in Libya), or any arrangement related to Megrahi dropping his appeal. Rejecting the PTA application, he argued, was appropriate because compassionate release was the legally correct mechanism given the specific terminal health circumstances.

The practical implementation of the decision was swift. Within hours of MacAskill's announcement, Megrahi, appearing visibly weakened and supported by officials, walked out of HMP Greenock. A carefully managed security operation facilitated his discreet transfer, likely by road convoy, to Glasgow Airport. There, an aircraft, widely reported to be a private jet provided by the Libyan government, awaited him on a secluded part of the airfield. He boarded the plane and departed Scottish soil, bound for Tripoli. His arrival in the Libyan capital later that day was a stark contrast to the sombre legal justifications offered in Edinburgh. Libyan state television broadcast extensive coverage of his return, showing large crowds gathered at the airport waving Libyan flags and pictures of Muammar Gaddafi. Megrahi, looking frail but managing a wave, was greeted effusively by senior officials, including Gaddafi's influential son, Saif al-Islam, who had played a key role in Libya's diplomatic rehabilitation efforts.

The reception was deliberately orchestrated as a triumphant homecoming, a vindication for a man Libya portrayed as unjustly convicted and wrongly imprisoned, finally returned through the persistence of the Libyan leadership. These images of celebration, particularly the waving of flags and apparent lack of remorse or solemnity, proved deeply offensive to many observers internationally, especially in the US, and dramatically fuelled the controversy surrounding the release decision.

The immediate reaction from the Pan Am 103 victims' families was intense, visceral, and heartbreakingly divided. Many family members, particularly the majority within the large US-based organizations, reacted with sheer fury, disbelief, and a profound sense of betrayal. They saw the release as an unforgivable act that trampled on the memory of their loved ones and undermined the very concept of justice. They condemned MacAskill's decision as politically motivated appeasement, driven by alleged secret deals for oil or trade, rather than genuine compassion. They pointed to the dropping of the second appeal as evidence of a backroom arrangement. They vehemently questioned the certainty of the three-month prognosis, predicting (correctly, as it turned out) that Megrahi would live much longer, and arguing the medical grounds were either flawed or manipulated. Their public statements expressed raw grief mingled with outrage directed at the Scottish Government, and also at the UK government for perceived complicity or failure to prevent the release. However, this was not the universal view. A significant number of families, particularly associated with the UK Families Flight 103 group and figures like Dr Jim Swire, expressed different perspectives. Some accepted the decision on purely compassionate grounds, believing it was wrong to force even a convicted murderer to die in prison far from home. Others, who harboured persistent doubts about the safety of Megrahi's conviction based on the SCCRC referral and the known evidential controversies, felt his release was justified, either because they believed him innocent or because his terminal illness made continued imprisonment seem pointless or cruel. This divergence of views, often reflecting different national perspectives and varying levels of confidence in the original trial verdict, created painful divisions within the already traumatized community of Lockerbie families, divisions that the release controversy only served to deepen.

The political fallout within the UK was immediate and severe. The Labour government of Prime Minister Gordon Brown, while constitutionally bound to accept the devolved nature of the decision, expressed strong disapproval. UK ministers, including Justice Secretary Jack Straw, indicated their clear preference had been for the Prisoner Transfer Agreement route, which would have seen Megrahi return to Libya but theoretically remain under sentence within the Libyan prison system. They criticized the Scottish Government for choosing compassionate release instead and complained about a lack of adequate consultation on a decision with such major international repercussions, particularly for UK-US relations. The Conservative opposition under David Cameron and the Liberal Democrats under Nick Clegg joined in condemning the decision, questioning MacAskill's judgment and calling for parliamentary inquiries into the circumstances surrounding the release, especially the allegations of links to trade deals. The Scottish National Party government, led by First Minister Alex Salmond, mounted a vigorous defence. They argued that Kenny MacAskill had acted properly and courageously within his statutory powers as Justice Secretary, applying Scots law and principles of compassion in a quasi-judicial manner, independent of political interference from London or Washington. They vehemently denied any connection between the release and oil contracts or any deal related to the abandoned appeal, portraying such accusations as baseless smears. The controversy dominated political debate in both Edinburgh and London for weeks, exposing tensions within the UK's devolution settlement regarding foreign policy implications of devolved decisions.

Internationally, the reaction from the United States government was one of unmitigated fury. President Barack Obama publicly stated the US "strongly disagreed" with the decision and called it "a mistake." Secretary of State Hillary Clinton registered deep disappointment. Attorney General Eric Holder condemned the release in particularly strong terms, calling it "an affront to the memory of the victims and their families." Perhaps most pointedly, FBI Director Robert Mueller, who as Assistant Attorney General back in 1991 had announced Megrahi's indictment, penned an open letter expressing his outrage and disappointment on behalf of the FBI agents who had dedicated years to the investigation. Across the US political spectrum, there was bipartisan condemnation. Members of Congress demanded explanations, threatened investigations, and called for punitive actions against Scotland or UK entities perceived as responsible. The allegations linking the release to a multi-billion dollar BP oil exploration deal with Libya, signed after diplomatic relations improved, became a major focus of US political and media attention, despite repeated, strenuous denials from BP, the UK government, and the Scottish Government, who all insisted there was absolutely no connection.

The incident caused significant diplomatic friction, straining the normally close relationship between Washington and London, and creating deep-seated resentment towards the Scottish Government in particular. The perception in the US was largely one of justice denied and national grief ignored, compounded by the celebratory scenes broadcast from Tripoli.

Libya, meanwhile, continued its carefully managed narrative. While celebrating Megrahi's return as a humanitarian triumph, the Gaddafi regime offered no official apology or acceptance of state responsibility for the Lockerbie bombing itself. Issues regarding substantial compensation for the victims' families remained largely unresolved at this point, requiring further protracted negotiations. The controversy over the medical prognosis also festered. As Megrahi continued to receive treatment in Libya and survived well beyond the initial three-month estimate (he eventually died in Tripoli in May 2012, nearly three years after his release), critics relentlessly cited this longevity as definitive proof that the compassionate release was granted on false or manipulated medical grounds. Supporters of the decision countered that predicting survival times for terminal cancer patients is notoriously imprecise, and survival beyond initial estimates does not invalidate the diagnosis or the compassionate principle applied at the time based on the best available medical advice. Nevertheless, Megrahi outliving his prognosis became a powerful symbol for those who believed the release was fundamentally illegitimate.

The compassionate release of Abdelbaset al-Megrahi remains a deeply polarizing and intensely debated event. It stands as a stark example of the complex, often agonizing intersection between law, medicine, politics, diplomacy, and raw human emotion. Kenny MacAskill's decision, defended by his government as a principled application of Scots law and compassion, was simultaneously condemned by powerful international allies and many victims' families as a betrayal of justice potentially influenced by other factors. It triggered a major diplomatic crisis, exposed fault lines within the UK's constitutional structure, deepened divisions among those most affected by the bombing, and generated a cloud of controversy and suspicion regarding the true motives behind the release that persists to this day. It ensured that even after the conviction and imprisonment of one perpetrator, the Lockerbie saga was far from over, destined to remain a source of enduring pain, argument, and unresolved questions.

Chapter 14: The Return and Final Years

The wheels of the aircraft carrying Abdelbaset al-Megrahi touched down on Libyan soil on the evening of August 20, 2009, marking the end of his physical incarceration in Scotland but simultaneously igniting a new, intensely controversial phase in the long saga of the Lockerbie bombing. His return, facilitated by the Scottish Justice Secretary's decision to grant compassionate release due to terminal prostate cancer, was framed by the Gaddafi regime as a triumphant homecoming, a moment of national vindication against perceived Western injustice. Yet, this carefully stage-managed event, broadcast globally, provoked outrage in the United States and the United Kingdom and deepened divisions among the families of the 270 victims. For Megrahi himself, now back in the embrace of his family but facing a bleak medical prognosis and remaining the sole individual convicted for the Pan Am 103 atrocity, the final years of his life unfolded against a backdrop of continued international scrutiny, profound political upheaval within Libya, and an enduring, desperate quest to overturn the verdict that defined his existence. His death in 2012 would ultimately close the book on his personal story but leave the central mysteries of Lockerbie frustratingly unresolved.

Return to Tripoli: Hero's Welcome or Quiet Decline?

The reception orchestrated for Megrahi upon his arrival at Tripoli International Airport was anything but low-key. Libyan state television cameras captured images of significant crowds gathered on the tarmac, waving Libyan flags and portraits of Muammar Gaddafi. As Megrahi, looking visibly frail and leaning heavily for support, emerged from the aircraft, he was greeted by senior figures, including Saif al-Islam Gaddafi, the dictator's son and heir apparent, who had positioned himself as a key architect of Libya's diplomatic re-engagement with the West, including negotiations related to Lockerbie. The symbolism was potent and deliberate: Libya was welcoming back its own, defying the Western powers that had imprisoned him, and implicitly rejecting the legitimacy of the Camp Zeist conviction. This portrayal, however, was met with international revulsion. US President Obama condemned the celebration, UK Prime Minister Gordon Brown termed it "repugnant," and victims' families expressed deep hurt and anger at what they perceived as a grotesque display lacking any sensitivity to their profound loss. The homecoming thus immediately highlighted the chasm between Libya's official narrative and the perception held by much of the rest of the world.

Following the public arrival ceremony, Megrahi was swiftly transferred to a Tripoli hospital for immediate medical assessment and treatment. The initial period after his return focused on stabilizing his condition and allowing him to reunite properly with his wife, Aisha, and their children, from whom he had been separated for over a decade, barring infrequent and difficult prison visits. Information about his subsequent life in Tripoli remained relatively controlled, disseminated primarily through occasional statements by family members, his lawyers, or brief, managed media appearances. He did not assume a public role or become a vocal political figure. Instead, reports suggested he largely retreated into the privacy of his family home, a substantial villa in a relatively affluent Tripoli suburb, where he lived under the continued protection and likely supervision of the Libyan state security apparatus. While technically a free man, his liberty was constrained by his severe illness and the ever-present security concerns surrounding such a high-profile figure. Access for international journalists was extremely limited and carefully managed, usually facilitated through his family or legal representatives.

Life for Megrahi in these years became an ongoing battle against advanced prostate cancer. He received continuous medical care in Libya, reportedly including hormone therapy and potentially chemotherapy, administered either at home or during hospital stays. His family consistently maintained that his illness remained severe and debilitating, pushing back against the intense international criticism fueled by his survival beyond the initial three-month prognosis cited for his compassionate release. They argued that while he had outlived the median estimate, this was not unusual in cancer cases and did not negate the terminal nature of his diagnosis at the time of release. This ongoing debate over the prognosis became a proxy war for the legitimacy of the release decision itself. Critics, particularly in the US, pointed to his continued survival as definitive proof of a flawed or manipulated process, possibly linked to alleged deals involving BP oil contracts. Supporters of the release decision, including some medical ethicists, countered that prognostication is inherently uncertain and that focusing solely on lifespan ignored the confirmed terminal diagnosis and the compassionate principles applied under Scots law. Megrahi's physical state, occasionally glimpsed in photographs showing significant weight loss and frailty, provided a somber counterpoint to the political arguments swirling around his longevity.

During this period, the Gaddafi regime continued its complex dance on the international stage. Having secured Megrahi's return and the suspension of UN sanctions, Libya pursued full normalization of relations and the lifting of remaining unilateral US sanctions. A major step involved finalizing comprehensive compensation agreements for the families of victims not only from Lockerbie but also from the UTA Flight 772 bombing and the La Belle disco bombing. These multi-billion dollar settlements, reached through intricate negotiations often involving complex legal structures and careful wording, allowed Libya to address outstanding claims and remove major obstacles to reintegration, but typically did so without issuing a formal, unambiguous admission of state guilt or responsibility for ordering the attacks themselves. Libya often framed these payments as accepting 'corporate' or 'civil' responsibility for the actions of its officials, a nuanced distinction that allowed them to settle claims while maintaining a degree of deniability regarding direct state-sponsored terrorism ordered from the top. Megrahi's presence in Libya, as the only convicted individual, remained a sensitive element within this broader diplomatic landscape. Meanwhile, the legal track continued, albeit slowly. Megrahi's lawyers pursued avenues related to his second appeal, potentially gathering further information or preparing arguments should his health have permitted, or planning for a posthumous continuation. Campaign groups like Justice for

Megrahi continued their work, publishing analyses critical of the trial evidence and lobbying for inquiries into the conviction's safety. Conversely, family groups convinced of his guilt remained vigilant, opposing any Libyan attempts to fully rehabilitate its image without full accountability.

Megrahi's Final Testimony?: Deathbed Claims and Unanswered Calls

The dramatic eruption of the Libyan Civil War in February 2011 fundamentally reshaped the context surrounding Megrahi and the Lockerbie case. As protests against Gaddafi's rule escalated into armed conflict and NATO intervened, the stability and authority of the regime that had secured Megrahi's release began to crumble. During the intense fighting, particularly the battle for Tripoli in August 2011 which led to the collapse of the regime, Megrahi's situation became precarious. Reports indicated he remained in his family home in Tripoli, severely ill and largely immobile, effectively caught in the crossfire. There were fears for his safety, concerns he might be targeted by anti-Gaddafi militias seeking retribution, or that victorious rebel forces might attempt to apprehend him, perhaps seeking to use him as a bargaining chip or even extradite him back to the West. However, amidst the widespread chaos and focus on capturing Gaddafi himself, Megrahi appears to have been largely left alone, his terminal illness perhaps rendering him a low priority in the violent struggle for control of the country. International media crews who gained access to Tripoli after its fall managed to locate Megrahi, finding him bedridden, extremely frail, and receiving basic care from his family, seemingly abandoned by the remnants of the collapsed state apparatus.

The fall of the Gaddafi regime initially sparked widespread hope that long-hidden truths about the Lockerbie bombing might finally be uncovered. The National Transitional Council (NTC), the interim governing body formed by anti-Gaddafi forces, made public statements indicating a newfound willingness to cooperate with international investigators and potentially grant access to the archives of Gaddafi's intelligence services. Figures like Mustafa Abdul Jalil, the former Justice Minister who defected and became head of the NTC, made headline-grabbing claims, asserting he possessed evidence proving Gaddafi personally ordered the Lockerbie bombing. Hopes were high that documents detailing the plot's planning, execution, and chain of command, potentially naming other individuals involved (including senior figures like Abdullah Senussi, Gaddafi's intelligence chief who was later captured), might finally be revealed. International investigative teams, including representatives from Scotland and the US, sought access to Libya to pursue these leads.

However, the reality on the ground proved immensely challenging. Post-Gaddafi Libya descended into prolonged instability, factional infighting, and near-statelessness in many regions. Establishing central control over government ministries and, crucially, securing the vast, sensitive archives of the former intelligence services proved extremely difficult. Records were likely dispersed, destroyed during the conflict, or deliberately concealed by individuals seeking to protect themselves or manipulate information. While some documents did surface, and various former officials offered competing narratives or accusations, no definitive, verifiable cache of evidence emerged that fundamentally altered the established understanding of the Lockerbie plot or provided conclusive proof either confirming Megrahi's guilt beyond doubt or fully exonerating him. The window for uncovering buried secrets, widely hoped for after Gaddafi's demise, largely failed to materialize amidst Libya's ongoing turmoil. During this period of national upheaval and his own rapidly declining health in late 2011 and early 2012, Megrahi gave what would be his final public statements, often through family members or journalists granted limited access to his bedside. His message remained unwavering: he insisted on his complete innocence, reiterated his claim that he was the victim of a grave miscarriage of justice, and expressed his dying wish that his name be cleared. He reportedly lamented his decision, made under duress due to his illness, to abandon his second appeal just before his release, believing that appeal held the potential to overturn his conviction based on the grounds identified by the SCCRC. He spoke of evidence he claimed his defence team possessed which would exonerate him, possibly contained within a manuscript or dossier he had been compiling. However, despite intense media interest, he offered no specific new revelations, no 'deathbed confession' naming others, no definitive clarification of the mysteries surrounding the plot. His final testimony to the world was a steadfast assertion of innocence against the weight of the guilty verdict that still legally stood against him.

Abdelbaset Ali Mohmed al-Megrahi died at his home in Tripoli on May 20, 2012, succumbing to the prostate cancer that had afflicted him for several years. He was 60 years old. He had survived for two years and nine months following his compassionate release from Scotland, far exceeding the initial three-month prognosis, a fact immediately seized upon by critics as final 'proof' of the release decision's flawed basis.

His funeral was held relatively quietly in Tripoli, attended primarily by family and friends, lacking the state fanfare that marked his return but still attracting significant local and international media attention. His death brought a formal end to his personal story but provided no definitive closure to the Lockerbie saga itself. Reactions were, predictably, divided along now familiar lines. His family mourned his passing, vowing to continue the fight to clear his name posthumously. The Libyan authorities expressed condolences but were largely preoccupied with internal struggles. Campaigners for his innocence declared that a man wrongly convicted had died without justice. Many victims' families expressed a sense of somber closure, acknowledging the end of a painful chapter, while others reiterated their belief in his guilt and expressed frustration that he had died technically a free man rather than in prison. Governments in the US and UK acknowledged his death factually, using the occasion to remember the victims and reaffirm the pursuit of justice for Lockerbie.

Megrahi's death left a legacy as contested and complex as his life and conviction. He remains the only individual ever found guilty by a court of law for the murder of the 270 victims of Pan Am 103. Yet, significant and well-documented doubts about the safety of that conviction, formally recognized by the SCCRC's referral for a second appeal which he never lived to pursue, persist within legal and academic circles and among sections of the public and victims' families. His death meant that crucial questions surrounding the evidence – the reliability of Gauci's identification, the exclusivity of the timer link, the potential non-disclosure of information – were never fully re-examined in an appellate court setting.

The alternative theories involving the PFLP-GC, Iran, and Syria, while officially discounted by the investigation leading to Megrahi's conviction, continue to be debated and explored by researchers and journalists, fueled by perceived geopolitical motives and remaining evidential ambiguities. Crucially, the question of who else within the Libyan hierarchy, potentially reaching up to Gaddafi himself, might have ordered, planned, or facilitated the bombing remains unanswered, despite tantalizing hints emerging after the regime's fall. Was Megrahi a lone operative (highly unlikely given the sophistication), a key player among others, or a designated scapegoat sacrificed to protect more senior figures? His death ensured he took any secrets he held about the wider conspiracy to his grave. The Lockerbie bombing thus endures not only as a horrific act of mass murder but as a case study in the immense difficulties of achieving universally accepted truth and justice in complex cases of state-sponsored terrorism, leaving behind a landscape of unresolved questions, enduring grief, and a conviction whose safety remains, for many, an open verdict.

Chapter 15: Voices of the Victims

The cataclysmic explosion that ripped Pan Am Flight 103 from the night sky above Lockerbie on December 21, 1988, was an act of terror whose immediate, violent impact lasted mere seconds. Yet, for the thousands of people connected by blood, marriage, friendship, or community to the 243 passengers, 16 crew members, and 11 residents of Lockerbie who perished, the explosion marked not an end, but the beginning of a lifetime irrevocably altered by loss, trauma, and a search for meaning in the face of calculated mass murder. As news reports filtered through – initially confused, then horrifyingly clear, filled with images of fiery devastation and widespread wreckage – families across the United States, the United Kingdom, and nearly twenty other nations were thrust into a nightmare of agonizing uncertainty, followed by the crushing confirmation of loss. Their loved ones, en route to festive reunions, returning from study abroad, engaged in business travel, or simply sitting in their homes on a quiet winter evening, had been violently torn from existence.

The Lockerbie bombing was not, for them, a distant news event or a complex geopolitical puzzle; it was a deeply personal wound, an intimate encounter with the brutal consequences of international terrorism that would shape their lives, galvanize them into action, forge profound bonds, create painful divisions, and fuel a decades-long, multi-faceted quest for justice, truth, remembrance, and ultimately, some form of peace.

Families Divided: Views on Guilt, Release, and Justice

In the immediate aftermath, the dominant emotions were shock, disbelief, and overwhelming grief. Families endured agonizing waits for official confirmation, desperately clinging to hope against mounting evidence. Many travelled immediately to Lockerbie, drawn to the epicentre of the disaster, needing to be near the last place their loved ones existed, however harrowing the scene. They encountered a small Scottish town reeling from its own trauma but offering extraordinary compassion, opening homes and hearts to strangers united in sorrow. Others converged on support centres established near major airports like JFK in New York or Heathrow in London, finding solace and information amidst fellow bereaved families. The specific nature of the disaster – the high-altitude disintegration, the violent dispersal of remains across miles of rugged terrain – inflicted a unique form of trauma. The process of victim identification was painstaking, protracted, and often harrowing, involving forensic experts piecing together fragmented remains, relying on dental records, fingerprints, and personal effects. For many families, the inability to have a complete body returned for burial added another layer of profound anguish to their grief.

This shared experience of sudden, violent loss under intense public scrutiny forged powerful initial bonds. People who were strangers just days before found themselves sharing hotel rooms, meals, tears, and information, creating an impromptu community bound by unimaginable tragedy.

From this crucible of shared grief and a rising tide of anger demanding answers, formal family advocacy groups quickly took shape. In the United States, which suffered the loss of 189 citizens, the primary organization became Victims of Pan Am Flight 103, Inc. (VPAF 103). Established within months of the disaster, it brought together hundreds of families, channelled their grief into action, and rapidly became a formidable lobbying force. Led by dynamic and articulate individuals often thrust into advocacy by personal loss – such figures as Bert Ammerman, a New Jersey principal who lost his brother Tom; Susan Cohen, a writer whose only child, Theodora, a Syracuse University student, died; Victoria Cummock, a determined advocate whose husband John perished; and numerous others who dedicated years to the cause – VPAF 103 pursued a clear agenda. They provided crucial mutual support and practical information to families navigating the complex aftermath. They relentlessly demanded answers from Pan Am regarding security lapses (eventually pursuing successful civil litigation against the airline) and pressed the US government for full transparency about pre-bombing intelligence warnings and the subsequent investigation. Above all, they campaigned tirelessly for the identification, apprehension, and prosecution of those responsible, becoming a constant presence in the corridors of power in Washington, ensuring that the victims were never forgotten and that political pressure for accountability remained high.

Their effectiveness stemmed from their moral authority, their organizational skills, and their unwavering determination fueled by personal loss.

Similarly, in the United Kingdom, families of British victims – passengers, crew, and the Lockerbie residents killed on the ground – formed UK Families Flight 103. Key figures emerged here too, including Reverend John Mosey, whose daughter Helga was on board; Dr Jim Swire, a general practitioner whose daughter Flora was a passenger, and who would become a prominent, sometimes controversial, voice questioning the official narrative; Pamela Dix, whose brother Peter died; and representatives from the Lockerbie community itself, like Maxwell Kerr, ensuring the voices of those impacted on the ground were heard. The UK group worked closely with its American counterpart, sharing information and coordinating lobbying efforts directed at the British government, Scottish authorities (including Dumfries and Galloway Constabulary and the Crown Office), and international bodies. While generally aligned in their core objectives, subtle differences in perspective sometimes emerged, perhaps reflecting the different legal and political contexts, or the unique experience of the Lockerbie community itself having lived through the immediate horror and recovery effort on their doorstep. Nonetheless, in the initial years, both groups presented a largely united front, demanding a thorough investigation and the pursuit of justice wherever the evidence led.

The announcement of the indictments against Megrahi and Fhimah in November 1991 was met with near-universal relief and validation among the organized family groups. It confirmed their belief that the bombing was a deliberate act of Libyan state-sponsored terrorism and offered the tangible prospect of a criminal trial. Throughout the long diplomatic standoff of the 1990s, this unity largely held firm. Both VPAF 103 and UK Families Flight 103 strongly supported the US and UK governments' insistence on extradition and backed the imposition and maintenance of UN sanctions against Libya as the primary means of applying pressure. Family members became adept lobbyists, regularly travelling to Washington, London, New York, and eventually The Hague, meeting with Presidents, Prime Ministers, Secretaries of State, Foreign Secretaries, UN Secretaries-General, and countless other officials. They provided powerful, often deeply emotional, testimony before parliamentary committees and congressional hearings. They organized vigils, press conferences, and awareness campaigns, ensuring the Lockerbie bombing remained a live political issue. Their collective moral pressure was instrumental in countering international 'sanctions fatigue' and resisting various Libyan attempts to broker deals that fell short of securing the suspects for a credible trial. They were a constant reminder of the human cost and the unwavering demand for legal accountability.

However, beneath the surface of this united front, differing perspectives began to emerge, particularly as the prospect of the unique trial at Camp Zeist neared and the complex, circumstantial nature of the evidence became more apparent. While the vast majority of families, especially within the powerful US contingent, remained firmly convinced of Libyan guilt and accepted the prosecution's narrative, a smaller but increasingly vocal group, predominantly associated with some UK families led by the articulate Dr Jim Swire, began to express profound doubts about the safety of the conviction, specifically against Megrahi. These doubts were fueled by several factors meticulously explored during the trial and appeal: the acknowledged inconsistencies and controversial aspects of Tony Gauci's identification evidence; the questions raised about the exclusivity of the MST-13 timer link to Libya, particularly surrounding the testimony of MEBO's Edwin Bollier; concerns about potential non-disclosure of relevant evidence by the prosecution or intelligence agencies; and a growing belief, informed by independent researchers and journalists, that the alternative theory involving the PFLP-GC, Iran, and Syria had been too readily dismissed by the official investigation, possibly for political reasons. This group argued that true justice required absolute certainty based on irrefutable evidence, and they believed the case presented at Camp Zeist failed to meet that standard.

Their quest shifted from solely demanding punishment for the named Libyans towards a broader search for the unvarnished truth, even if it pointed towards different perpetrators or revealed uncomfortable realities about governmental actions. This divergence led to painful public disagreements and sometimes strained relationships between family members who had previously found solace in unity. The definition of "justice" itself became contested terrain – was it achieved by the conviction secured at Camp Zeist, or did it require a deeper, more conclusive uncovering of the entire conspiracy, regardless of where that path led?

The compassionate release of Megrahi in August 2009 blew these existing fissures wide open, creating deep and lasting divisions within the Lockerbie family community. For the majority, particularly the American families represented by VPAF 103, the decision was met with incandescent rage and a profound sense of injustice revisited. They saw it as a political act disguised as mercy, a betrayal of the legal process, and an unbearable insult to the memory of their loved ones. They vehemently rejected the compassionate grounds, citing Megrahi's subsequent longevity as proof the medical prognosis was flawed or manipulated. They embraced theories linking the release to secret UK government deals facilitating BP's oil exploration contract with Libya, viewing it as a morally bankrupt trade of justice for commercial gain.

Their public statements condemned Scottish Justice Secretary Kenny MacAskill in the strongest possible terms and expressed deep disappointment with both the Scottish and UK governments. Conversely, the smaller faction, including Dr Swire and others primarily within the UK group, took a starkly different view. Believing Megrahi to be innocent, they saw his release, given his terminal illness, as the only humane and morally correct course of action, arguing it was wrong to let a potentially innocent man die in prison far from his family. Even among those UK families who did accept Megrahi's guilt, some expressed a degree of understanding for the decision based on principles of compassion inherent in Scots law, separating the legal verdict from the question of mercy in the face of terminal illness.

This stark divergence – between outrage demanding retribution and perceived justice undone, and a complex mix of doubt about guilt, belief in compassion, or focus on truth over punishment – created lasting scars. Public spats erupted between leading figures from different family factions, reflecting the deeply personal and irreconcilable nature of their perspectives, forever shaped by how they interpreted the evidence, the verdict, and the meaning of justice in the long shadow of Pan Am 103.

The Ongoing Campaign: Seeking Truth and Accountability

The conviction and later death of Abdelbaset al-Megrahi did not signify an endpoint for many families. For those convinced of his guilt, his death in Tripoli brought a measure of closure, albeit one tainted by the controversy of his release and the fact he died technically free. For those convinced of his innocence, his death represented the tragic end of a man wrongly convicted, intensifying their determination to clear his name posthumously and uncover what they believe to be the true story. And for many families across the spectrum, the fundamental desire for a complete understanding of how and why the bombing happened, including the identification of all involved, particularly those higher up the chain of command, remained unfulfilled. Consequently, the decades following the trial have seen continued, albeit increasingly diverse and sometimes divergent, campaigns focused on truth, broader accountability, remembrance, and ensuring lessons were learned.

The legal battle surrounding Megrahi's conviction continued posthumously. Following the SCCRC's 2007 referral based on grounds suggesting a potential miscarriage of justice, and Megrahi's own abandonment of that appeal prior to his release, his family, supported by campaigners, lodged further applications with the SCCRC. This culminated in a second referral by the Commission back to the High Court in March 2020. The SCCRC again cited grounds related to unreasonable verdict and non-disclosure, finding that Megrahi might have been denied crucial evidence at his trial. This led to a posthumous appeal heard in late 2020 and early 2021 on behalf of Megrahi's family. However, in January 2021, the High Court Appeal judges rejected this second appeal, upholding the original conviction once more. Despite this legal setback, campaigners associated with the Justice for Megrahi movement continue to argue the case remains unsafe, analyzing evidence, publishing critiques, and calling for a full independent inquiry into the conviction and investigation. Their persistence highlights the enduring nature of the doubts surrounding the official verdict for a significant constituency. (Self-correction: Incorporating the latest legal status accurately as of early 2025 is crucial here - the second appeal was indeed rejected in 2021).

Separately from the criminal case against individuals, the pursuit of accountability from the Libyan state unfolded primarily through complex negotiations over financial compensation. Driven largely by pressure from the US government under intense lobbying from American family groups, Libya eventually agreed in the early 2000s (around 2003) to a landmark compensation package totalling approximately $2.7 billion.

This fund was intended to compensate the families of all 270 Lockerbie victims (as well as victims of other attacks attributed to Libya). The agreement was intricately linked to the phased lifting of remaining UN and unilateral US sanctions, providing Libya with a path towards international rehabilitation. Under the deal, Libya accepted "responsibility for the actions of its officials" but carefully avoided a direct admission of guilt for ordering the bombing. While this legal distinction was significant for Libya, the payment of substantial compensation (reportedly up to $10 million per family, paid in stages) provided crucial financial redress for the bereaved families, acknowledging their suffering and loss in a tangible way. For many families, accepting the compensation was a pragmatic decision, necessary for rebuilding lives and securing futures, though some maintained that no amount of money could substitute for full accountability and truth.

Amidst the legal battles and political campaigns, the vital work of remembrance continued unabated, driven by the families' determination that the 270 victims should never be reduced to mere statistics in a geopolitical conflict. Significant memorials now stand as permanent tributes. In Lockerbie, the town most directly scarred, the Garden of Remembrance adjacent to Dryfesdale Cemetery offers a tranquil space for reflection, featuring a simple stone wall engraved with the names and nationalities of all 270 victims. Within the cemetery itself lies a dedicated plot where unidentified or unclaimed remains recovered from the crash site are interred. In the United States, the Lockerbie Cairn at Arlington National Cemetery, built from 270 blocks of red sandstone gifted from a quarry near Lockerbie, serves as the primary national memorial.

Syracuse University, forever linked to the tragedy through the loss of 35 of its students returning from study abroad, created the moving Place of Remembrance on its campus, featuring a wall listing the names, and established the Remembrance Scholarships, awarded annually to honour the victims by supporting current students. Countless other smaller memorials – plaques, gardens, stained-glass windows, benches – exist in communities across the globe touched by the tragedy. Annual memorial services, held faithfully every December 21st at Lockerbie, Arlington, Syracuse, and elsewhere, provide recurring opportunities for families to gather, share their grief, honour their loved ones, and reaffirm their collective commitment to remembrance. These acts ensure the human cost of Pan Am 103 remains visible and serves as a caution for future generations.

Perhaps the most concrete, life-saving legacy driven by the families' advocacy lies in the realm of aviation security. Horrified by the demonstrable failures that allowed a bomb to be checked through three international airports onto Pan Am 103, family groups became relentless campaigners for improved safety measures. Their persistent lobbying of governments, airlines, and international aviation bodies throughout the 1990s was directly responsible for driving major reforms. Mandatory 100% passenger-baggage reconciliation (Positive Bag Match or PBM systems) became standard practice for international flights, aiming to prevent unaccompanied bags from travelling. Investment surged in developing and deploying advanced Explosive Detection Systems (EDS) capable of automatically screening checked luggage for plastic explosives, moving beyond the limitations of 1980s X-ray technology. Air cargo and mail security protocols were significantly tightened.

Background checks and access controls for airport employees were enhanced. International cooperation and intelligence sharing regarding aviation threats improved markedly. While the security landscape was further transformed after 9/11, the fundamental changes implemented in the decade following Lockerbie, largely due to the families' refusal to accept the status quo, created a significantly more secure global aviation system. This enduring legacy of enhanced safety, potentially saving countless lives, stands as a powerful, positive outcome born from their devastating loss. The families of Pan Am 103, through their decades of grief, advocacy, internal struggles, and unwavering commitment, remain central to the Lockerbie narrative – their voices a constant reminder of the human cost, their actions shaping the quest for justice, truth, and a safer world.

Chapter 16: The Enduring Lockerbie Question

More than thirty-six years have elapsed since the night sky over Lockerbie, Scotland, was torn apart by the fiery disintegration of Pan Am Flight 103. In the intervening decades, an immense global effort has been expended in the pursuit of answers and accountability. A painstaking investigation, unprecedented in its scale and international scope, pieced together fragments of wreckage and forensic clues. An extraordinary diplomatic confrontation led to years of sanctions against Libya, culminating in a unique compromise: a Scottish trial held on neutral Dutch soil. That trial resulted in the conviction of one Libyan intelligence agent, Abdelbaset al-Megrahi, for the murder of 270 people, while his co-accused, Lamin Khalifah Fhimah, was acquitted. Megrahi's conviction withstood a rigorous appeal process, but he was later controversially released from his life sentence on compassionate grounds due to terminal cancer, returning to Libya where he died protesting his innocence in 2012. The regime that allegedly sponsored him, led by Muammar Gaddafi, eventually fell in a violent revolution, sparking hopes for new revelations, hopes largely unfulfilled amidst subsequent chaos. Libya paid billions in compensation to victims' families, accepting civil responsibility while stopping short of admitting direct state guilt for ordering the attack. And in a significant recent development, another alleged Libyan operative, Abu Agila Mohammad Masud Kheir Al-Marimi, accused of assembling the bomb, was indicted by the United States and extradited to face trial, adding yet another complex layer to the legal aftermath.

Yet, despite this long and tortuous history – investigation, sanctions, trial, conviction, appeals, compensation, regime change, a new indictment – the Lockerbie bombing refuses to settle into the quiet certainty of a closed historical chapter. Fundamental questions about the evidence, the investigation, the trial's verdict, and the full extent of responsibility remain subjects of intense debate, rigorous academic scrutiny, persistent journalistic inquiry, and deeply felt division among those most affected. The "Lockerbie Question," encompassing a constellation of doubts, ambiguities, and unanswered calls for truth, endures, a potent symbol of the profound challenges in achieving universally accepted justice and definitive understanding in the face of catastrophic, state-sponsored terrorism.

Beyond Megrahi?: Re-examining Evidence and Intelligence Failures

The legal status of the Lockerbie case in early 2025 is formally clear yet deeply contested in practice. Abdelbaset al-Megrahi remains the only individual ever convicted for the bombing. His conviction was upheld by the Scottish Court of Criminal Appeal in 2002. A subsequent referral of his case back to the High Court by the Scottish Criminal Cases Review Commission (SCCRC) in 2007, based on six grounds suggesting a potential miscarriage of justice, led to a second appeal attempt that was ultimately abandoned by Megrahi himself prior to his compassionate release in 2009. A further posthumous appeal, initiated by his family following a second SCCRC referral in 2020 (again citing grounds including unreasonable verdict and non-disclosure), was definitively rejected by the High Court in January 2021.

Thus, under Scots law, Megrahi's guilty verdict stands. Lamin Fhimah remains acquitted. Meanwhile, the prosecution of Abu Agila Masud on charges related to his alleged role as the bomb-maker is proceeding through the US federal court system, representing an active, ongoing effort to pursue further individual accountability. Yet, beneath this formal legal surface, the controversies that plagued the original investigation and trial persist with undiminished intensity, fuelled by detailed critiques of the core evidence.

The identification of Megrahi by the Maltese shopkeeper, Tony Gauci, remains perhaps the most significant and persistently troubling aspect of the conviction. While the trial judges acknowledged flaws, including Gauci's exposure to media photographs of Megrahi before the crucial identification session, they ultimately deemed his testimony sufficiently reliable when corroborated by evidence placing Megrahi in Malta. However, critics, including the SCCRC in its referrals and numerous legal commentators, argue this conclusion stretched the principles of corroboration and eyewitness reliability beyond acceptable limits. Decades of psychological research have demonstrated the profound suggestibility of eyewitness memory, particularly when exposed to external influences like media reports or repeated questioning over long periods. Gauci's documented inconsistencies regarding the date of purchase (shifting significantly over time before aligning with dates Megrahi was allegedly in Malta) and his description of the purchaser raise fundamental questions about the accuracy of his recollection.

The defence argument that the pre-trial identification procedure was fatally tainted, rendering the subsequent in-court identification effectively worthless, continues to resonate strongly. Added to this are the lingering questions surrounding the multi-million dollar reward offered for information leading to conviction, which, critics argue, created at least the perception of a potential financial motive influencing Gauci's testimony, regardless of his denials. For many sceptics, the conviction of Megrahi rests too heavily on this single, deeply problematic eyewitness account, which they believe should have been ruled inadmissible or, at minimum, insufficient to overcome reasonable doubt. The appeal courts' deference to the trial judges' assessment of Gauci's credibility, despite the acknowledged flaws, remains a central point of contention for those who argue a miscarriage of justice occurred.

Similarly, the forensic evidence linking the MST-13 timer fragment exclusively to Libya, while accepted by the courts, continues to be challenged. The complex and often contradictory testimony of MEBO co-founder Edwin Bollier regarding his company's security, record-keeping practices, potential modifications to timers, dealings with other clients (including East German intelligence), and even alleged thefts of timers, provided fertile ground for defence arguments that the claim of exclusive supply to Libya could not be proven beyond reasonable doubt. While the prosecution presented invoices and testimony supporting the Libyan contract, the defence highlighted ambiguities and inconsistencies that, they argued, undermined certainty. Independent researchers have also pointed to potential alternative sources for similar timing technology or questioned the absolute certainty of the forensic match based on such a minuscule fragment recovered months after the devastating crash and extensive environmental exposure. The chain of custody of the fragment itself, from its discovery amidst wreckage to its analysis in various laboratories, has also been subject to scrutiny, with critics raising hypothetical possibilities of contamination or misidentification. While the courts ultimately accepted the timer evidence as a powerful link, the surrounding complexities and Bollier's problematic testimony ensure it remains a focus of ongoing debate for those questioning the safety of the conviction.

The narrative tracing the unaccompanied bomb suitcase from Malta through Frankfurt to Heathrow, while providing a coherent theory for the prosecution, also relies on a chain of inferences about security lapses rather than direct proof. Fhimah's acquittal underscored the lack of direct evidence linking anyone to the illicit introduction of the bag at Luqa. The defence successfully argued that opportunity did not equate to proof, and alternative interpretations of Fhimah's actions were possible. Likewise, the arguments regarding security failures at Frankfurt and Heathrow relied on demonstrating systemic weaknesses and procedural gaps in 1988, but lacked definitive proof that the specific bomb suitcase exploited these gaps on that particular day. The complete absence of any direct forensic evidence – fingerprints, DNA, fibres definitively linking Megrahi or Fhimah to the suitcase, radio, Semtex, or timer – remains a striking feature highlighted by critics. They argue the entire suitcase journey narrative, while plausible, remains a circumstantial construct vulnerable to reasonable doubt, particularly when considering alternative possibilities for how the bomb might have entered the system, perhaps even at Heathrow itself through an insider or a different security breach entirely unrelated to the Malta connection.

These perceived weaknesses in the case against Megrahi inevitably keep alive the alternative theory focused on the PFLP-GC, potentially acting for Iran with Syrian facilitation. Proponents of this theory meticulously point to the PFLP-GC's documented expertise in building barometric bombs hidden in Toshiba radios (strikingly similar to the Lockerbie device), the powerful Iranian motive following the USS Vincennes' downing of Iran Air 655, the location of key PFLP-GC cells in Europe (particularly Germany), and specific intelligence reports from the period allegedly linking these actors to planned attacks on American aviation targets. They highlight the 'Autumn Leaves' operation in Germany just months before Lockerbie, where such bombs were seized, as evidence of active plotting. Critics of the official investigation argue that crucial intelligence pointing towards this axis was potentially ignored, downplayed, or even suppressed, possibly due to shifting geopolitical priorities (e.g., the West seeking Syrian cooperation against Iraq in the lead-up to the 1991 Gulf War). They question whether the timer fragment was truly unique to Libya or if similar components might have been accessible to other groups. While the official investigation and subsequent court decisions concluded the evidence against Libya was more compelling, the PFLP-GC/Iran/Syria theory remains a persistent counter-narrative, sustained by documented facts and unanswered questions about the investigation's focus and comprehensiveness.

This leads to broader concerns about potential intelligence failures or manipulations. Were pre-bombing warnings, beyond the vague Helsinki alert, received but not adequately disseminated or acted upon by US or UK intelligence agencies?

The families certainly pursued this question vigorously in the early years. More significantly, were intelligence agencies entirely forthcoming during the investigation and trial regarding information they held about alternative suspects or potentially exculpatory evidence related to Megrahi? The SCCRC's referrals for Megrahi's second appeal cited concerns about non-disclosure by the Crown as a key ground, suggesting potentially relevant information might not have been available to the defence at the original trial. The inherent secrecy surrounding intelligence operations makes definitive answers elusive, but the possibility that crucial information was withheld, whether deliberately or inadvertently, continues to fuel doubts about the fairness and completeness of the judicial process.

Even setting aside doubts about Megrahi's individual guilt, the question of wider responsibility within the Libyan state remains profoundly unresolved. The Camp Zeist judges themselves concluded the bombing had the hallmarks of a state-sponsored operation, implying involvement beyond the two individuals in the dock. Suspicion has long centred on senior figures like Abdullah Senussi, Gaddafi's intelligence chief, and on Gaddafi himself as having likely authorized the attack. The fall of the regime in 2011 offered a tantalizing prospect of uncovering documentary proof or securing testimony from former insiders. While some claims emerged, including from the former Justice Minister Mustafa Abdul Jalil directly implicating Gaddafi, concrete, verifiable evidence establishing the full chain of command has not been forthcoming, hampered by Libya's subsequent instability and the likely destruction or concealment of sensitive records.

The US indictment of Abu Agila Masud in December 2020, alleging he was the technical expert who actually built the bomb under JSO direction, represented a significant attempt to pursue further accountability. Masud's subsequent apprehension in Libya and transfer to US custody in December 2022 to face trial marks a potentially crucial development. The US indictment alleges Masud worked closely with Megrahi and others within the JSO, and his prosecution (ongoing as of early 2025) could yield vital new information about the conspiracy's inner workings, potentially corroborating Megrahi's role while also implicating others more clearly. However, until Masud's trial concludes, and perhaps even afterwards, the full picture of who ordered, planned, financed, and facilitated the Lockerbie bombing within the Libyan state apparatus remains incomplete, a major unanswered part of the enduring Lockerbie question.

Legacy of Terror: Lessons Learned and Lessons Ignored

The enduring legacy of the Lockerbie bombing extends far beyond the unresolved questions surrounding the criminal investigation and trial. It remains deeply embedded in the lives of the thousands of family members who lost loved ones, shaping their experiences and actions for decades. Their journey, from the initial trauma through years of campaigning for justice, truth, remembrance, and reform, is a testament to extraordinary resilience. While divisions emerged over time regarding the verdict and subsequent events, their collective refusal to allow the victims to be forgotten, their relentless pressure on governments and international institutions, and their dedication to memorialization have profoundly shaped the Lockerbie narrative and its consequences. The memorials in Lockerbie's quiet Garden of Remembrance, beneath the imposing Arlington National Cemetery cairn, on the Syracuse University campus, and in numerous other communities, stand as powerful, permanent tributes, ensuring the human cost of this act of terror remains visible and honoured. Their voices, individually and collectively, continue to demand that the lessons of Lockerbie are not ignored.

One of the most significant and tangible legacies lies in the transformation of global aviation security. The horrifying realization that a sophisticated bomb could be successfully smuggled onto a major international flight through multiple airports exposed critical systemic failures. Driven by the tireless advocacy of the victims' families, who channeled their grief into demands for concrete action, governments and the aviation industry implemented sweeping changes throughout the 1990s. Mandatory 100% passenger-baggage reconciliation systems (Positive Bag Match - PBM), designed to prevent unaccompanied luggage from flying, became standard international practice. Massive investment flowed into developing and deploying advanced Explosive Detection Systems (EDS) and Explosive Trace Detection (ETD) technologies capable of screening checked baggage far more effectively than the rudimentary X-ray machines of 1988. Air cargo and mail screening protocols were significantly strengthened, recognizing these as potential vectors for attack. Airport perimeter security, employee background checks, and airside access controls were tightened considerably. International cooperation and intelligence sharing on aviation threats were enhanced through organizations like the International Civil Aviation Organization (ICAO).

While subsequent events, notably the 9/11 attacks, revealed different types of vulnerabilities and led to further revolutionary changes (particularly regarding passenger screening and cockpit security), the foundational improvements in baggage and cargo security implemented directly in response to the Lockerbie bombing represented a quantum leap forward, undoubtedly preventing subsequent tragedies and creating the layered security architecture that passengers experience today. This life-saving legacy remains a direct result of the lessons learned from Pan Am 103 and the families' refusal to accept inaction. However, the evolving nature of terrorist threats – new explosive types, methods of concealment, potential for insider threats, cyber-attacks, drones – means constant vigilance and adaptation remain essential, raising the question of whether the 'Lockerbie mindset' of proactive security improvement is always maintained.

Lockerbie also offers enduring, if complex, lessons about international justice and dealing with state-sponsored terrorism. The eventual trial at Camp Zeist, while controversial, stands as a rare example of individual criminal accountability being pursued, and partially achieved, for a major act of state-sponsored terror through a civilian court process, albeit one requiring extraordinary diplomatic compromise and legal innovation. It demonstrated the potential power of sustained international sanctions coupled with patient diplomacy in eventually compelling a pariah state to cooperate, up to a point. However, the decade-long standoff, the compromises required (neutral venue, no jury), the contested nature of the evidence, the split verdict, the compassionate release controversy, and the failure to secure accountability beyond one potentially mid-level operative highlight the immense difficulties involved. Holding sovereign states truly accountable for sponsoring terrorism, as opposed to prosecuting individual agents, remains a profound challenge under existing international law. Lockerbie serves as a case study in the complex interplay between the pursuit of legal justice, the realities of geopolitical interests, and the limitations of international institutions when confronting defiant states. Did the response ultimately deter other potential state sponsors? Or did Libya's ability to withstand sanctions for so long, secure its agent's release, avoid explicit admission of guilt while paying compensation, and descend into chaos unrelated to Lockerbie sanctions, send a more ambiguous message? The answers remain debated among international relations scholars and policymakers.

Ultimately, the Lockerbie bombing endures as a powerful, tragic symbol carrying multiple layers of meaning. It represents the horrific potential of terrorism to strike indiscriminately, shattering ordinary lives on a massive scale. It symbolizes the intricate challenges of international investigation and the often-elusive nature of achieving universally accepted justice. It stands as a testament to the extraordinary resilience and advocacy of victims' families determined to find meaning and create change from unimaginable loss. It serves as a cautionary tale about the potential fallibility of legal systems and the importance of rigorous scrutiny of evidence, particularly in highly politicized cases. And it remains shrouded in enduring mystery, with fundamental questions about the full conspiracy, the ultimate responsibility, and the complete truth likely destined to remain unanswered definitively.

The "Lockerbie Question," therefore, is not a single query but a constellation of unresolved issues that continue to demand attention, ensuring that the bombing of Pan Am 103 remains more than just a historical footnote – it is an ongoing narrative about loss, justice, truth, and the enduring search for accountability in a world still grappling with the legacy of terror.

Epilogue: Echoes in the Present

More than thirty-six years now separate the present day from that terrible night in December 1988 when Pan Am Flight 103 was violently erased from the sky above Lockerbie. A generation has grown to adulthood under the long shadow cast by the bombing and its complex, often agonizing aftermath. The world itself has undergone profound transformations – the Cold War ended shortly after the tragedy, the landscape of international terrorism shifted dramatically following the attacks of September 11, 2001, geopolitical alliances have reshaped, and the nation identified as the perpetrator state, Libya, experienced revolution, collapse, and ongoing fragmentation. Yet, despite the relentless passage of time and the seismic shifts in global affairs, the Lockerbie bombing refuses to recede quietly into history. Its echoes continue to reverberate in courtrooms, in diplomatic corridors, in academic debates, in the ongoing work of campaigners, and most profoundly, in the lives of the thousands of individuals forever bound together by the shared trauma of loss. As we stand in early 2025, the Lockerbie saga remains stubbornly incomplete, a narrative marked by a single, contested conviction, enduring questions, and the persistent, fundamental human need for truth and comprehensive justice.

The legal landscape surrounding Lockerbie, while seemingly settled in some respects, gained a significant new dimension in recent years. Abdelbaset al-Megrahi, the only person ever convicted for the bombing, died in Tripoli in 2012, his conviction having been upheld through Scotland's primary appeal process, and a final posthumous appeal attempt failing in 2021. For the Scottish legal system, his guilt remains the official finding, though heavily contested by many who point to the acknowledged flaws in the evidence highlighted by the Scottish Criminal Cases Review Commission.

Lamin Fhimah, Megrahi's co-accused, remains acquitted, living freely since his return to Libya in 2001. For years, it seemed the judicial chapter might be closed, leaving broader questions of state responsibility and the roles of others unanswered. However, in December 2020, the US Department of Justice unsealed charges against a third alleged conspirator, Abu Agila Mohammad Masud Kheir Al-Marimi, identified as a senior Libyan intelligence operative and explosives expert who allegedly assembled the bomb device itself. This development was monumental. In a move that surprised many, Masud, who was reportedly imprisoned in Libya following the fall of Gaddafi on unrelated charges, was transferred into US custody in December 2022. As of this writing in April 2025, Masud is awaiting trial in a US federal court in Washington D.C., facing charges related to the destruction of Pan Am 103. This ongoing prosecution represents a renewed, active effort to achieve individual accountability for the bombing. Its potential significance is immense: Masud's trial could corroborate key aspects of the original narrative regarding Libyan involvement and the Malta origin, potentially shed new light on the roles of Megrahi and Fhimah, and possibly provide evidence *implicating higher-level figures within the former Gaddafi regime, including the still-imprisoned intelligence chief Abdullah Senussi. Conversely, his defence will undoubtedly challenge the evidence, potentially reigniting debates about alternative theories or investigative flaws. The Masud case ensures that Lockerbie, far from being solely a matter of historical record, remains a live legal issue, holding the possibility, however uncertain, of further revelations and judicial findings.*

Yet, the quest for truth extends beyond the confines of courtrooms. The fall of the Gaddafi regime in 2011 briefly ignited hopes that Libya's extensive intelligence archives might finally be opened, revealing the unvarnished story behind the Lockerbie plot – definitive proof of who gave the order, the full extent of the conspiracy, and potentially settling the debates about alternative theories or Megrahi's precise role. These hopes, however, have been largely frustrated by Libya's subsequent descent into protracted instability and civil conflict. Access to reliable information remains extremely difficult, state institutions are fragmented, and the security situation hinders any systematic search for or verification of historical records. While fragments of information and accusations from former officials have occasionally surfaced, no comprehensive, verifiable account has emerged from Libyan sources. Similarly, campaigners continue to call upon the UK and US governments to declassify potentially relevant intelligence files, arguing that greater transparency is needed to fully understand the context, the warnings, and the potential missteps surrounding the bombing and its investigation. The enduring secrecy surrounding certain aspects of the case fuels suspicion and allows competing narratives to persist.

The full truth, in all its likely complexity, remains elusive, possibly buried forever in inaccessible archives or the memories of individuals now deceased or unwilling to speak. For the families of the 270 victims, the passage of decades has not diminished the pain of their loss, but their journey has evolved. They remain the living heart of the Lockerbie story, their experiences shaping its legacy. The initial unity forged in grief gave way over time to differing perspectives on justice, accountability, and the safety of Megrahi's conviction, leading to painful divisions that persist today. Some remain steadfast in their belief in the official verdict, finding solace in Megrahi's conviction and focusing on remembrance and ensuring the lessons learned lead to a safer world. Others remain equally convinced of a miscarriage of justice, continuing the arduous fight to clear Megrahi's name and uncover what they believe to be the hidden truth, often centred on alternative perpetrators. And many perhaps exist somewhere in between, grappling with enduring uncertainty while focusing on honouring the memory of their loved ones and finding personal peace.

Their shared commitment to remembrance remains a powerful unifying force, manifested in the poignant annual memorial services and the permanent memorials that stand as testament to the lives cut short. Their advocacy, born from tragedy, has undeniably left a lasting, positive legacy in the realm of significantly enhanced aviation security, making air travel demonstrably safer for subsequent generations. Yet, for many, the lack of complete, universally accepted answers means true closure remains perpetually out of reach. Their resilience is extraordinary, but their continuing quest, in its various forms, underscores the profound, long-lasting human impact of mass casualty terrorism.

Lockerbie's echoes also resonate in the broader contexts of international law and counter-terrorism. The case stands as a complex precedent in the effort to hold state actors accountable for sponsoring terrorism. It demonstrated the potential of sustained international pressure, combining sanctions and diplomacy, to eventually compel a pariah state towards a form of legal reckoning. The innovative Camp Zeist trial model, while unique and controversial, offered a pragmatic solution to an otherwise intractable jurisdictional standoff. However, the case also exposed the limitations: the difficulty of securing conclusive evidence against secretive regimes, the potential for political considerations to influence legal processes, the challenges of achieving justice acceptable to all stakeholders, and the lack of robust mechanisms to ensure full state accountability beyond individual prosecutions or negotiated compensation deals. In the post-9/11 world, the approaches to counter-terrorism have evolved further, often involving military intervention, targeted killings, or different legal frameworks like military commissions. Yet, the fundamental challenges highlighted by Lockerbie – balancing justice with security, navigating state sovereignty, ensuring fair trials while protecting intelligence sources, and addressing the root causes of state-sponsored violence – remain acutely relevant in the 21st century.

The bombing of Pan Am 103 serves as a crucial, albeit deeply troubling, case study in this ongoing global struggle. Therefore, as we reflect in April 2025, the Lockerbie bombing is far more than a historical tragedy confined to the late 1980s. It is an active legal case, with the Masud prosecution potentially rewriting or reinforcing key aspects of the narrative. It is an ongoing source of pain and activism for hundreds of families still seeking answers and remembrance. It is a subject of continued academic and journalistic investigation, challenging official narratives and probing persistent anomalies. It is a potent symbol in international relations, reminding us of the devastating consequences of state-sponsored terror and the complexities of achieving justice across borders. The enduring Lockerbie question is not merely about the guilt or innocence of one man, or the precise mechanics of the plot, but encompasses broader themes of truth, memory, accountability, and the capacity of legal and political systems to respond effectively to mass atrocity. While some answers have been provided, many remain elusive, perhaps permanently obscured. The echoes of that December night continue to be felt, a solemn reminder of lives lost, justice pursued but perhaps incompletely realized, and the enduring human quest for understanding in the face of profound darkness.

Printed in Great Britain
by Amazon